PARALYZED BY PERFECTION

Made By ~~Mistakes~~

ANN-MONIQUE BAILEY HUTCHINSON

PARALYZED BY PERFECTION. Copyright © 2021 by Ann- Monique Bailey Hutchinson.

All Rights Reserved. Printed in the United States of America. No part of this book may be used or reproduced, stored in a retrieval system, or transmitted in any form or by any means except for brief quotations in critical articles or printed reviews without the prior written permission of Ann- Monique Bailey Hutchinson and O.Y.R. Books & Publishing.

Unless otherwise indicated, all Scripture quotations are taken from the Holy Bible, American Standard Version, New King James Version, and King James (American Version).

Cover Design by O.Y.R. Books & Publishing
ISBN- 9798633848625
First Edition: April 2021

From Me to You

To:

From:

Your story can change lives. Live it, record it, and then share it for the difference it can make.

Love, Ann-Monique

TABLE OF CONTENTS

Dedication 7

Thank You 8

Foreword 10

'Preamble' 13

Chapter 1 15

Those Moments And That Time 15

Chapter 2 27

Made By 'Mis-Takes' 27

Chapter 3 41

The Thought Life 41

Chapter 4 53

Stuck On Fear 53

Chapter 5 67

Angry Birdie 67

Chapter 6 78

Outside In 78

Chapter 7 92

Likes, Views, Comments! 92

Chapter 8	107
Third-Party Rights	107
Chapter 9	118
Ctrl+ Alt+ Delete (Control Issues)	118
Chapter 10	128
Growing In The Cracks	128
Reference	142

Dedication

For my Mommy, Marlene Bailey, may I inherit even a drop of her strength and for my Father, Norman Bailey, the most humble soul I have ever known.

I wrote this book because you both raised me to believe that I can do anything to which I commit my mind. Mommy, you bought me my first book, and you may not know it, but that purchase inspired me to begin my writing journey. Daddy, you have been my and our family's quiet strength for all my life, and you deserve every bit of love I can give. You have both pushed me to be the best version of myself, believing in me even when I gave up on myself. You have unashamedly and selflessly invested in me and continue to do so to date. In time, I pray I become the greatest I can be, but either way, I know you will both be proud of me forever and always. I love you both infinity.
And to all imperfect souls in this race called life, you will be okay.

Thank you

Completing this book was more challenging than I ever imagined, but with the help of a great support system, *"it is finished."*

I am who I am because of God Almighty. So without hesitation, I thank Him for this gift of storytelling with which He so graciously blessed me. Without Him, I would not be able to accomplish this milestone.

Leroy N. Hutchinson, my husband… the one who finally pushed me to complete this project; I thank you so much. You are the extra motivation I needed and the best company for making it through late-night writing struggles. Thank you for reminding me of my first love of writing and actively pushing me to finish what I started so long ago.

I am immensely grateful to my editor, Mrs. Gail Harvey, who greatly impacted the finished product now available to the world. You did an excellent job of editing this candid journey and provided perfectly timed guidance along the way. I look forward to working together on many more projects.

Thank you ever so much, Minister Dr. Heidi

Leith, for writing the foreword for this project. You were able to relate so well to my journey, and in doing so, you meticulously conveyed the message behind this book through the foreword.

To my publisher, O.Y.R. Books and Publishing, thank you for being an integral part of this process. I could not have asked for a better publisher.

To my cousins who allowed me to share a chapter in their journey, thank you, ladies. I know your stories will impact others positively.

Foreword

There are many ways to get a message across to persons, but if our efforts fail, we often get irritable and feel as if we are being ignored. There are also many roads that we can take to arrive at our desired destination. While they all have bumps, corners, and even detours called disappointments and mistakes, we will eventually arrive at our destination if we are persistent. Regardless of the road we travel, our response to and ability to recover from the challenges we face will determine our level of success.

I can identify with the author, having had my own unexpected life-changing experience. My story changed when I fell in love with and married a wonderfully saved, caring, and thoughtful young man. This was not a mistake or an ordinary encounter! God knew, and I later realized that it was not an *"oops..."* but a call to serve God and serve people. Like the author of this book, my wedding day changed everything. I live my life on purpose, knowing that God has His hands in my journey, even when I make 'mistakes'; I always trust His wisdom, knowing His plan for my life is perfect.

Ann-Monique Bailey Hutchinson has accomplished significant milestones along the journey of becoming who she wants to be. It is clear that she had to grapple with the many decisions and make independent judgments about what she heard and saw. From the pages of this book come 'life lessons' with the encouragement to live successfully in a challenging world by ordering our priorities and keeping them in line with God's priorities.

We have all dreamed at some time, but have you braved the obstacles and opposition and allowed the Lord to use you to realize those dreams? I challenge you to let each chapter of this book speak to your dreams. Let them address your "what ifs" and prepare your mind and heart for the possibilities. A trail is marked for you on each page of this book. Allow your passion to start an unquenchable fire in your belly, grow the courage to move forward because fear must not win.

The author challenges her readers to have confidence

in God regardless of their journey and obstacles present along the way. She encourages us to hold on to our dreams because God has the power to perform any miracle.

Minister Dr. Heidi P. Leith
Public Relations Director
Church of God of Prophecy, Jamaica

'Preamble'

In the summer of 2017, for the first time in my Twenty-Six years on planet Earth, I felt like my life had come to a complete halt. Nothing was working out as planned. I had resigned from my first job as an Attorney-at-Law. I was questioning whether I wanted to go back into law. In general, I felt stuck, as if I was going through life with darkly tinted shades over half-blinded eyes. The thought that life was not going according to my perfectly laid out plan gave me actual nightmares. I was in a hard place, so I had to ask myself some tough questions, which I now ask of you.

What could you have done if you were not afraid of making mistakes? What could you now do if you were not awaiting your idea of the perfect moment? Picture the life you could have if, for once, you pushed aside the taunting voice of fear, the need to be perfect at all times, and the urge to put off everything until circumstances are such that you believe nothing could go wrong.

Oh, the great possibilities! The images caused my heart to dance with giddy exhilaration. This represented the freedom to be and to do anything as long as God would have it to be so.

Finishing this book gave me that free feeling of fulfilment. I overcame myself and my internal struggles enough to complete a journey that started three years ago in a season of uncertainty, pain, and fear. Eventually, I realized that the thing we are most afraid of doing is that very thing that will set us completely free. That is what my story, **Paralyzed by Perfection: Made by Mistakes,** aims to do. It maps my unravelling, my healing, and my growth. For you, this book will offer reassurance that despite making mistakes, despite failures that might come as a result of these mistakes, growth and hope reside amid these imperfect moments.

Even if you don't get it right tomorrow, sleep again and do it again until you've mastered the art of trying, living, fighting, and giving yourself a chance to survive without getting everything right and without being perfect in this world full of imperfections.

Chapter 1

Those Moments and That Time

"No time is ever the perfect time...except morning, noon or night." - **Ann- Monique Bailey Hutchinson**

What if we could control time? What if we could add or minus hours to or from the day as we see fit? If this were possible, let us imagine this ability is indiscriminately assigned to each human on the earth, regardless of age, gender, class, or origin. Wouldn't we have to consult with everyone else in the world before making that final decision, or would we proceed, with our selfish plans being the sole concern at the time?

As humans, we are inherently selfish; that is, we naturally put our very own interests ahead of the welfare of others. With time and the increasingly fast pace of life came two popular thoughts, *"too little time"* and *"not the right time."* With these realities in mind, if we had the free will to manipulate time as we saw fit, many would probably do it to ensure that our plans are actualized. When given a certain amount of power, a particular type of control, the 'human' in us often lose perspective. The ability to control time would fall under the umbrella of "a certain kind of power." A more valuable resource than time, one can hardly find. A more wasted one, perhaps only God's grace, and money would rival. Not surprisingly, any control over this precious resource would drive the best of us to limits only God could understand.

In reality, only God controls time; only God can determine the right versus the wrong time, so let us step back from the images painted earlier. That was me merely casting the net. Now that I have reeled you in, let me remind you that the perfect God we serve lives inside, outside, before, and after time. He is father time, not Stan Lee's 1963 comic book superhero *"Doctor Strange."* No doubt, the real issues with time rest within us as imperfect humans. I can admit this now, especially as I acknowledge that perfection is unattainable in this life.

Between Time and I

I have always considered myself to be quite busy. Then came March 16, 2019, the day everything about me, including my very name, changed. My wedding day. This day meant I would have to make a drastic adjustment in many areas of my life, including my use of time. I may discuss this momentous day later in this candid journey, but for now, I freely admit that for many years, time and I had a rocky relationship. I have always wanted to ensure that I met deadlines or arrived at places at the right time, especially since I hated being the center of attention. These are not bad things. *As an aside, if you want all eyes on you, be the last person to arrive at a function. I promise that you will be the center of attention.*

When I was younger, the struggle with time included determining when to study for exams versus closing the novels and going to bed. There was also the struggle to turn the television off and get some well-needed sleep or when to pay attention in class and stop writing another high school drama in my notebook instead of notes (fun times, I tell you*).* There were times (*there goes that word again*) when I struggled with saying the right thing at the 'right time,' breaking up with someone at the 'right time,' ending a call at the right time. The list was endless.

The struggle did not diminish with age. To date, I am still learning that as important as time and timing are, there is no greater enemy to getting things done than the belief in the phrase *"not the right time."* On April 7, 2020, I suggested to a relative whose journey I was familiar with that she write a book or journal about her journey to date as a Covid-19 lockdown project. I knew she had an exciting story. In her usual mature but slightly amused tone, she said, "*I'm thinking *about it."*

I tried to convince her, *"I'm telling you it can happen. I see others starting and finishing books. It is possible."*

She laughed a little, but seconds later, firmly reiterated, *"It can happen, but not now."*

I sighed, though she was not able to see me, *"So what are you waiting on?"*

My heartbeat slowed momentarily as the words I was guilty of overusing came right back to haunt me the moment she said, ***"The right time."***

That phrase! It will be the death of many of us and our dreams! When I read the text message, it was one of those *"O.M.G."* kinds of moments, primarily because I had just completed this chapter about the "right time" issue. Of course, I edited this chapter after that chat with my cousin. How many of you have said that to someone or had someone say that to you? How often do we change our minds after making a decision? Sometimes we do so after a suitably painful kick in the nether parts by a well-meaning friend or family. Most times, the right time never happens, and that is the heart-breaking reality we all face. I encouraged her to write; I reminded her there is no better time than now to make her plans or commence an action. I told her that cancelling our plans to wait on time is like waiting on a male to become a man in the womb. It cannot happen.

We are not talking about a broken watch or other timing device giving the incorrect reading here. We are talking about moments, some defining, others merely passing. Whether they change your life or change from day to night, all and every moment is important. One should adequately think of them all as the *"perfect moment"* or the perfect time or timing. I believe that if there were only one moment for everything in life, many of us would be walking shells by this time, empty of hope, since we all have missed out along the way. Thank God for grace, I say! Thank God for second, third, fourth, and many chances. The presence of these second chances is not an excuse to waste those first opportunities. Unless God does something about it, undoubtedly, we will miss out.

'Timely' Regrets

There are *'those moments'* and *'that time'* which we would all like to relive, to capture forever and encase in the perfect photo frame. Then there are *'those moments'* and *'that time'* which we believe we missed out on and can never get back. The feeling of regret, which follows in the latter circumstances, can be blinding, if not emotionally paralyzing.

Indubitably, our regrets are often our most significant hurdles, preventing the present from becoming. More often than not, our regrets keep us connected to our past and always wondering about our future. They are like metal collars around the neck, holding you captive to what could have been but was not. I have found myself in this situation on too many occasions to call it a comfort zone. It is everything I described above and then some. Naturally, such intense feelings of regret would flow from one who believed a moment was missed and also thought he/she missed the only moment. Many books remain unwritten because a prospective author felt he or she didn't write about the issues before others did; because he or she believed himself or herself to be too old; because the timing was simply not the right time.

Many wives blame their husbands for their failure to travel the world when they were younger. In contrast, some husbands blame their wives for not giving them the space, time, and support necessary to start a business. Some parents blame their children for poor timing because they came when Mommy and Daddy wanted to focus on their tertiary education. In casting blame, many fail to focus on the desired outcome or goal beyond the moment they initially believed was the best moment.

I submit that the perfect time is maybe morning, maybe noon, or possibly night. The ideal time is whenever you have the opportunity! Whenever God says to go at it, not when you do all you think you need to do to prepare for it! The right time is the time you had and continue to have to remain on this earth. The time does not expire and become 'null and void' unless God says that the time for you to do this thing is over. I learned this the hard way often. What it means mostly is that we have to use the time we have when we have it. Anything can happen at any time. I believe we have to actively accept this reality and divorce the ancient belief that it is too little too late to become.

Joanne Rowling, known more popularly by the pen name J.K. Rowling, conceived the *Harry Potter* series while she was travelling on a four-hour delayed train trip from Manchester, England, to London, England. While she was writing the book, her mother died from Multiple Sclerosis (M.S.). Her marriage ended in divorce, and she became jobless. She, along with her child, depended on state benefits. Her situation became so bad; she later described her economic status as *"poor as it is possible to be in modern Britain, without being homeless."* Twelve publishers rejected the first in the series of seven books before Bloomsbury, a publishing house in London, England, finally published the book. Harry Potter, now worth about Fifteen Million United States Dollars (US$15,000,000.00), is a global brand. As of May 2019, J.K. Rowling's net worth was approximately One Billion United States Dollars.

Very few individuals would dare to say she wrote the book at the right time. One could hardly imagine a more imperfect and difficult time. Yet, it propelled her into fortunes most people will never dream of in their lifetime. The point here is not to motivate one to riches. Instead, I hope to remind someone that bathing in regrets and pain about missed opportunities will cause one thing; missing additional opportunities.

Time is one of the most unpredictable elements in life. Yet, the Bible reminds us that for us as humans, time is not infinite. Will I find the same fortunes as J. K. Rowling if I publish one or two of the over forty books I have completed or started since 2001? Yes, you read it correctly. I have written over forty fiction books and about four non-fictions, either in my notebooks, notebooks my brother discarded, folder leaves in binders, phones I have lost, or my laptops and desktops.

As a child, I often battled with the grand dream of becoming a published and best-selling author; I wanted to become the next Danielle Steele or James Patterson. Conversely, along with my thoughts of grandeur came my realities, much like fraternal twins of the opposite sex. I was one of four kids from a family of six, with parents struggling to make ends meet. My parents did not have connections to publishers or financiers. I was too young, too shy, and it was simply *not the right time.* At least, those were my thoughts of my reality. Nineteen years later, except for my Wattpad account and now this book in your hand, I have published none of the books I spent hours writing, pouring out parts of me that no longer seem of interest at this stage of my life.

I was limited by what was more than my reality; my thoughts and lack of resources limited me. In the year 2017, this book finally dropped in my thoughts. I wrote the chapters and chapter summaries in an old notebook, which I have since misplaced. Then I met my husband, who published five books since we met, and still, I did not publish a single book. I even completed additional books while we were dating and before he published his first book. In these circumstances, one could undoubtedly conclude that I have wasted time and an abundance of opportunities.

Were there regrets? There were some, but there were also lessons, another close friend of time. The faster we learn the lessons teacher time has to teach us, the easier it will be to use the remainder of the time God gave us. Time wasted can never be regained. Let it no longer be said that you have been waiting on the *'right moment'* or the perfect set of circumstances.

Seasons

According to the wise man Solomon, *"to everything, there is a season and a time to every purpose under the heaven."* *(Ecclesiastes 3:1)* The scripture states that there is a time to do everything, a time to live and to die. Do we allow ourselves to 'die' while waiting on the right time, our *'right'* time, and not God's? This chapter does not aim to disagree with the word of God. The key to this chapter is always to remember that we do not determine our seasons; God does. Unless He says so, wait no more. The time to become is now. The time to chase after that dream God has placed in your heart is not tomorrow, not when things get better, not when you meet *'Mr. Right'* or *'Mrs. Right.'* Do it while you have time; time is life, so live it, use it. No time is perfect than the present. You will come to appreciate life just a little more when you realize just how well you used the 2,207,520,000 seconds you may naturally live on this earth, strength, and grace aside.

Timely Reminders
1. Time is always present.
2. Time is Life; use it.
3. Time waits on no man.
4. Time has no regrets.
5. No time is perfect than the present.

Chapter 2

Made by 'Mis-takes'

"We make mistakes, and mistakes make us."- **Leroy Hutchinson**

Once upon a time, I feared the very mention of the word *'mistake.'* It held a sinister, dark, and scary connotation that caused people like me, who struggled with the need to be on point or right at all times, to endeavor to practice social and physical distancing protocols with anything that sounded, felt or looked like a mistake.

Enter my husband, Leroy Hutchinson, a Minister of Religion, Youth Pastor, Author, Financial Advisor and Entrepreneur. Naturally, many young people confided in him about their various struggles. While he did not disclose said problems, I, too, would often ask him for tips on how to deal with other young people also going through their seasons. Like him, I was a Youth Director in the Church of God of Prophecy, Jamaica.

While sharing tips and tricks of the trade with me, he would tell me that when a young person said to him, *"I made a mistake,"* a general follow-up question would be, *"how did it happen?"* One standard answer would be, *"I don't know."* He would gently instruct the person to reconsider the question and his or her responses. He reminded him or her that mistakes do not just happen. The role he or she likely played in the process would have imparted knowledge. The tips would continue, but from these conversations, I have been able to better understand that there is more to mistakes than what one usually considers on the surface. I concluded that in many cases, if not on your journey but mine, one of three things creates that resulting mistake: I was misinformed, misdirected, or I misinterpreted a portion of or all the surrounding circumstances.

Ironically, it is easy to lay the blame at the cross of Jesus for not preventing us from doing silly things. Realistically, it is far easier to cast the full extent of the responsibility on those closest and dearest to us. However, while the actions or inactions of others play a part in our reality, this God-given gift called *'choice'*... is pivotal. Yes, some things happen to us without warning, allowing us little or no time to prepare ourselves. We can hardly take the blame for the results of such occurrences. Our response to such circumstances is just that, our response. Therein exists the choice; how we respond. For these reasons and many more, it is integral that we choose carefully what we take in, where we go, who we want to follow, and generally, what we take away from all the above.

Take 1 - Misinformation

We often find ourselves in various uncomfortable positions because of misinformation. Whether that misinformation makes or breaks us depends on you as individuals and the circumstances of the entire situation.

In or around January 2010, I was in my final year of high school, what we call the upper sixth form in Jamaica. While I was no social butterfly, nor am I that now, I had a few friends in or close to my age group. I was applying for University without the knowledge of my parents. Eventually, I informed them of my intentions. I had no idea if I could ever attend because, as far as I knew, my parents could not afford what seemed like a luxury to me. However, I still wanted to try. I finally decided on the degree I wanted to pursue, a Bachelor of Laws Degree from the University of the West Indies (U.W.I.) Mona, Jamaica.

I spoke to someone with similar ambitions about my intended course of studies. I sought his help with the application process. When our conversation ended, my dreams of becoming the first person from my household to pursue a university degree and to become an Attorney-at-Law were dashed. My friend told me two things. He told me that I needed a first degree before applying for the degree. Secondly, he said the University did not accept sixth-form students who more than likely did not have a first degree. I was devastated, and I was ignorant —error number one. I failed to check the facts; I failed to call the University; I did not do what any mature eighteen-year-old in a similar position would have done. I was very naïve. That was a door closed in my face. It hurt like my mouth did when a fellow schoolmate and I fought in primary school (or grade school), and she knocked my teeth out. *Fret not; it was already loosened.*

When I finally applied for University, I applied to read for a degree in the Faculty of Humanities and Education. I needed to submit certain documents to the Student Administration Services (S.A.S.). A female employee checked my documents when I dropped them off. She came to me and asked, *"What is it that you really want to study? With these grades, are you sure this degree is it?"*

I was a shy, awkward kid; still, a spark of hope raised its beautiful head somewhere on the inside. Could it be that she had something meaningful to say?

I quietly informed her, *"I want to study Law, but a*

friend of mine told me that I needed to have a Bachelor's Degree first, and I don't. Plus, I can't afford it." The lady gently cleared up the fog of ignorance that had tightly enveloped my head for some time, telling me there was no such rule or barrier. She encouraged me to maintain the grades I had or do even better. We spoke about the degree and faculty that I truly desired and the subjects and grades that I had obtained to date. We had a lengthy discussion, and at the end of it, I left S.A.S. feeling hopeful. There was hope, not a certainty, but a glimmer of possibility. I could do something about my dreams, after all.

Mistake number two, I did not take this lady's information, and to date, I still regret it. I would love to let her know the life-changing role she played in my educational journey —the power of a conversation. Sometime later, someone told me that my friend succeeded in applying to the Faculty of Law, U.W.I., Mona. When I heard about the application, I felt the pain of betrayal like it was a physical assault on my body. It felt like that moment when my fourth or fifth-grade classmate, a misguided boy who I hold nothing against today, kicked me in the ear. Fortunately, I did not hurt for long. Shortly after, I also received my letter of acceptance to the U.W.I. on the Government Sponsored Program.

This program allowed me to study for one year of my Law Degree in Jamaica and two years in Barbados, with a large percentage of my tuition covered by the Government. A few months later, I was awarded the Grace Kennedy Foundation Scholarship for 2010. The foundation stuck with me to the end of Norman Manley Law School in 2015. I continue to be grateful for these blessings, for Grace Kennedy Group, a gift that keeps on giving to so many others to date. My educational journey is a constant reminder that God has a wonderfully exciting sense of humor.

I nearly allowed misinformation to determine my first step into the tertiary arena. Note the presence of the word "allowed." I know and accept that I contributed to this misstep. I also acknowledge that, but for God stepping in at the most appropriate time, shuffling the deck of cards, restarting the game, shifting the tides, I would be living a different life. I could not say whether I would be better or worse off if I had continued along the path of Humanities and Education. However, I now understand that despite the difficulties, *"all things work together for good to those who love the Lord, to those who are called according to His purpose (Romans 8:28).*

I have also learned that whether or not someone contributed to your storm or painful moments, holding this against the offender will hinder you, never him or her. Getting back at such a person may seem like a good option, but not for the individual who sees an opportunity to learn and, by learning, to grow. My almost three decades on this earth have so far taught me quite a few lessons. In this take, I have proven that those who are most willing to retain a positive outlook on a set of circumstances will eventually climb up the step of their errors, over every single bridge of misinformation and closer to the best version of self and season. This positive outlook is by no means without its challenges. However, the other side of positive is depression, fear, anxiety, doubt, worry, what-ifs, and perfection paralysis. Choose you this day which you will serve, because whatever controls you and your products, to that you are a servant.

Take 2 - Misdirection

In some theatrical productions, some performers will seek to have their audience's attention drawn away to one thing, to distract it from another. Without a doubt, this is a form of deception. Similarly, we, too, are drawn away by small yet life-changing artifices. This issue reminds me of the Decepticons in the movie 'Transformers.' The Decepticons are the main antagonists in the fictional universe of the Transformers franchise. They are a faction of sentient robotic lifeforms led by Megatron, identified by a purple face-like insignia. These Decepticons and the other transformers evidence the fact that what we see is not always what we get. Along the way, we will meet up on numerous forms of deceptions, but whether we defeat the Megatrons we face depends on the will of God for our lives.

Misdirection often results from misinformation. Earlier, misinformation shifted my gaze from what I wanted to what seemed attainable, based on my limitations. I immediately took my eyes off my future and focused instead on the dictates of my circumstances. My heart was broken but was well enough to grab hold of my realities and make it work, although a degree in the Humanities and Education faculty was not what I wanted out of life.

My decision to accept those circumstances as my

future meant that I settled, albeit for what was not a terrible thing. It was a change in direction, but it was still a degree. I would still make my family proud. I could do well just the same. Who knows? After falling ill, to the point of hospitalization in pursuit of my Legal Education certificate in 2014, I may well have done better health-wise. My actual path took a toll, but my possible path never happened. It was merely a possibility, but I thought it was my final destination.

Before the acceptance letter came, my parents had accepted that I might not become the Lawyer that everyone in the family who knew me well enough thought I would be. At least they wouldn't have to worry about finding Ten Thousand United States dollars for three years, true? God had other plans for me, though, and Grace Kennedy Foundation did not hesitate to play its role.

Life is packed with seasons, and these seasons can change, some faster than others. The less time one spends looking at the wrong thing or travelling down the wrong path, the more possible it is for one to look away, turn back and kick-start the correct journey. Unfortunately, there are no undo buttons in this life that bring you back to the place where you started.

There are no take-backs, but second chances are abundant.

There are other opportunities. One cannot spend forever looking at what was, or even what is. If one spends too much time doing so, one might miss what could be. Balance plays an integral role in the script of life. My family and God were my balance, a balance I needed at that point in my life. What is your balance? What are those Decepticons that can either make you or break you? We must identify these early because failure to note the latter can often result in delays and, sometimes, abortions. Timing will forever wrap itself around every aspect of our lives, but this is a reality we must all come to accept as the norm. So while people's actions can throw us a curveball, our immediate actions or inactions can add to the scuffle. It behooves us well to see ourselves as integral in the ultimate path our journey takes.

God will not come down and shove us in the right direction. We must follow the clues He gives us ever so often through people and circumstances and, most importantly, in His words. The journey is worth it, far more than taking out our anger at ourselves or others for not being and doing what we would have preferred. Optimus Prime asked it this way; *"Are you going to let it all happen again for something as useless as revenge?"* Nay, not at all.

Take 3 - Misinterpretation

The one who understands what is said or done more readily can also keep the peace. However, peace will rarely result from one failing to grasp what another is trying to release. Very few things annoy me more than explaining a million times what I believe is a relatively straightforward situation. It is irksome, but it reminds me that I could work a little harder on my patience. Despite the realization that a dam could break when one fails to hear what is being said or done, misinterpretation in various areas of our lives increases without fail. Yet, life continues. Everything happens, and still, so does life.

Unfortunately, life is not like WhatsApp, allowing users to delete a message before the recipient reads it. Whatever we say or do now will generally yield a result either simultaneously or soon after the word or action. It makes sense then that we give the best at the first instance.

Some circumstances lead to more frequent

occurrences of misinterpretation than others. I believe it is more likely to happen when one is tired or under pressure. Additionally, it may occur when dealing with unresolved personal issues or instability in the thought life. It is often the result of inadequate or poor communication and can also result from ignorance and past experiences. I believe the text lingo "k" and "ok" by themselves are not only crude but sometimes disrespectful. It shows in my mind thoughtlessness and zero effort by the author of the message. It has a tone that often sounds dismissive and uninterested. These are my take-away from the phrase, but I have discussed the same with people who seem genuinely surprised at my conclusion. Could I be wrong about it? Yes! Most assuredly. Could I be right? Sometimes, yes, but how I respond to the author will once again reflect on me, not the author.

The point is, some people read for context and content; others read for grammar. The perfectionists (formerly me, I am declaring) miss opportunities looking for how things are written; the grammar, the errors, the flaws, instead of the context and the content. I am learning slowly that the above matters, in some cases, more than others. We would all like to get things right and always be on point. We can try, but I hope that in trying, we remember that what we are aiming for is the best product or service from ourselves, not the best compared to others or not a perfect product or service. There is, after all, nothing wrong with having high standards.

Made for you

Perfection has no company on this earth because it simply isn't." **Ann- Monique Bailey Hutchinson**

Chapter 3

The Thought Life

"Be Careful how you think; it might just become you and you, them."- **Ann-Monique Bailey Hutchinson**

IF our thoughts could be used against us in the court of law or the court of public opinion, what would you be guilty of? Which offence would you be caught with your pants down committing quietly? I imagine that some of us would be on trial for the murder of taxi drivers and other drivers, especially in rush hour traffic. No stones here! Some parents would be behind bars for the beating death of a disrespectful child. Divorce rates would be reduced even as 'spouse on spouse' crimes increase. There would be a rapid rise in the conviction rate for the growing number of employers being found dead in the least expected places. We thank God that our thoughts alone cannot lead to our criminal conviction. This world would look like a much different place if that were the case. This route is not my usual one. It caused me to pause for a while and do some introspection. People rarely think about what they are thinking about. I was writing this down, and it still sounded a little strange.

While it forms a large part of who we are, few people spend time pondering what their minds are usually focused on, mainly because life is often busy. Our thoughts often aggressively shove us to get with it, to get things done, because failure to do so has consequences.

We are not strangers to the reality of rising early to get ready for the day ahead, and as the day progresses, we focus solely on the tasks at hand. While some can concentrate on the task at hand, others struggle with what seems like the simple task of focusing on their immediate responsibilities. There are many distractions in our lives. I posit, however, that our thoughts are one of the most significant distractors.

Have you ever had the experience of trying to get someone's attention, but she is so lost in her thoughts, she cannot hear you? So powerful is the grip of her thoughts her physical reactions are hindered completely by something she cannot see. Take it further and try to touch such a person. I can recall seeing the startled movement of that individual suddenly being released from the controlling arms of the invisible boss in her head. We spend hours of our lives lost in the woods of our thoughts, carried away with fear and anxiety. *"Should have," "could have,"* and unrealism often dictate how we respond to our reality. For those who are engaged in a daily battle with their thoughts, which like white-collar criminals, seek to rob them of their peace, responding to reality becomes a separate struggle.

What if we made a habit of doing frequent mental audits? It would be to our advantage to check in on our thought life, taking deliberate steps to address our thoughts. Most importantly, we should learn to control these thoughts, which, more than we like to admit, often control us and how we respond to others.

Mental Audit

When you can pause or at least slow down and begin a detailed assessment of your mental state, history, and trend of thoughts, then you can better grasp the truth of your thought life. I refer to this as a mental audit. What happens between our two ears, in that slightly over three pounds organ, can affect as little as our moods and as much as our physical health. I have travelled both roads. Our thoughts can be our silent cheerleader as much as they can be that deafening bomb that explodes into our demise, to our surprise. We must be prepared to take control of such powerful weapons.

In 2 Corinthians 10:5, Paul says, *"casting down arguments and every high thing that exalts itself against the knowledge of God, bringing every thought into captivity to the obedience of Christ."* If our thoughts were irrelevant to our wellbeing, I doubt the Lord would address the issue through Paul.

I have fought a private battle with my thought life, and it baffled me that I could be saying one thing, and my thoughts would be challenging me with the opposite of what I was saying. I meant what I said or what I did, but then came a thought, questioning my decisions, wondering, fearing, *'what iffing,' 'should having.'* Anxiety naturally flows from this struggle. When you are anxious, you can also become sharp with those around you, causing unintentional tension and hurt. As the struggles of trying to get everything right continue, so do the number of things that go wrong. Murphy's Law succinctly puts it like this, *"everything that could go wrong, will go wrong."*

I recall more than one occasion where I became lost in the web of my thoughts while driving to or from the court. Talk about living dangerously. I often reflected on what was to come or what transpired in court on my journey across Jamaica. I would completely *'zone out,'* a dangerous tendency for a young driver, for any driver. I have never had an accident, but I've had to grab the steering wheel with both hands to realign the vehicle—very close calls.

I remember the rush of fear that enveloped me when I realized that I was so out of it that I might have missed a pedestrian if he or she was crossing the street. If a car were immediately in front of me, I would have crashed into the back. If there was an emergency, I would have missed it completely, to my detriment and that of other drivers or road users. If this battle only occurred around the steering wheel, that would be one thing. I have sat among friends and missed lines of conversations, absorbed in my thoughts, asking questions of the past, fearing the present, and worrying about my future. The only things that those thoughts challenged were my ability to engage productively in the present, dissatisfaction with the past, and constant anxiety about the future.

Over a decade ago, my teacher taught me a beautiful verse of scripture while attending the Port Morant Primary and Junior High School in St. Thomas. When I win the battle against my thoughts, I think about my thoughts and visualize the danger zone I have ventured into. I do so with the reminder from the scripture in Philippians 4:8, which says, *"Finally brethren, whatever things are true, whatever things are noble, whatever things are just, whatever things are pure, whatever things are lovely, whatever things are of good report if there is any virtue and if there is anything praiseworthy – meditate on these things" (Phil 4:8).* It does not get more direct than this as for guidelines, at least not for me. So when I shift my train of thought, which takes deliberate effort, the fear of failure and anxiety are naturally replaced. I can testify to feeling peace and a willingness to accept the present for what it is after I do this.

It becomes easier to prepare mentally for what comes because of the hope that rises when one thinks about pure things, lovely things, and good reports. How could positive energy not follow when positivity is sanitizing the mind? I now know that whatever we feed our thoughts, our thoughts will reproduce. When we feed our minds pure, noble, and praiseworthy food, it naturally gives birth to like results.

In her book, **'*Switch on Your Brain,*'** Dr. Caroline Leaf said, *"As we think, we change the physical nature of our brain. As we consciously direct our thinking, we can wire out toxic patterns of thinking and replace them with healthy thoughts."* Is the battle an easy one? No. Do we always win with our thoughts? No. As much as I would love to claim this perfect record, no one always wins at anything. I am considering my journey with perfectionism issues as I say this. God Almighty is the only exception. John Maxwell wisely said, *"Positive thinking may not always change our circumstances, but it will always change us."* So then, we ask ourselves, is it worth winning this battle with our thoughts? Do we want to change despite our circumstances? Yes, absolutely yes. This win definitely needs to be a win.

What do you think?
It is easy to conclude that if one struggles with their internal thought process, they may also struggle with what others think about them. Indeed, the results may vary based on individuals and each individual's circumstances. An internal struggle rarely stays internal permanently and will reflect in our external circumstances and interactions more often than not. Either way, an internal or external struggle prohibits forward movement either wholly or in part. For some, the battle is apparent, but for others, it is a subtle taunt almost. You know it exists but in denial, you pretend it does not.

During my time at Calvary Basic School (elementary

school), I stood out for all the wrong reasons. My teachers struggled with me because though I excelled at my book work, my interpersonal relationship with the students, especially male classmates, was messy. Now that I have outgrown that season of my life, I was proud to let one teacher, Miss Gayle, know that all her efforts were not in vain; that all those complaints made to my mother were not in vain.

As young as I was, I battled two things that caused me to isolate myself physically, socially, and emotionally from those around me while at school. The first was something my mother and my maternal grandfather often reminded me of. I now know they did it with intentions to protect me, telling me regularly to *"stay away from boys."* The second was the way some kids, especially the boys, treated me. I was young, but I was clever, so I understood that I was being marginalized. I realized that I was being bullied when some would call me *"fatty"* and *"the black one."* I was taller and, yes, way darker than most of my classmates.

When I look back at my graduation photograph, I was certainly a little on the chubbier side. My graduation picture reflected what I recall feeling even then, at a tender age; I was angry, miserable, moody, and annoyed. I was not too fond of school. I could hardly wait for the driver to collect me when school was dismissed each day.

As I write, I recall the frown on my sweaty but cute, chubby face on many occasions at that stage of my life. In my young mind, I believe I had some inkling of what my fellow schoolmates thought of me, and as a child, it affected how I saw myself. If only I understood then what I do now. Had I only believed what my mother tells me even now, how beautifully and uniquely created I was. I knew I was a brilliant child, I heard that regularly, but I also listened to my classmates' words and saw their actions.

I learned at an early age that kids could be cruel to each other. My struggle then was both internal and external, and this made the journey difficult. It affected my self-esteem. I saw myself through the mirror of their eyes and their words, and what I saw, I did not like.

If only I knew then what I know now. If only I knew that the presence of struggles did not mean the absence of purpose. I wish I had known that pain did not mean the lack of growth. I was barely five or six years old. If

I saw things as I do now, I would tell my kid self to chin up. I would say that a symbol of strength was allowing oneself to be stretched but not broken. I would let her know that the stretching brings growth spiritually, mentally, and emotionally.

Purposeful Thinking

Life is much like a long movie with many scenes, most of them filled with you, the main character, getting whooped by one villain after the other. Fret not. It is not all bad. There are highlights along the way once you refocus those inner struggles, adjust mentally, and expand the thought process. Allow the mind to relax, and know that your final choice can make the outcome better or worse.

Our thought life is the secret evidence that could be used against us in our *'own'* court of reality because how we think consistently becomes who we are. If you believe that you are less than others, you will live this reality. If you think you are better than others, pride will become your closest friend. A healthy and bold mind is the aim. We cannot fear our thoughts or fear sharing them with someone else other than our journals. Who knows, our *'foolish'* thoughts may change the very nature of our employers' businesses. It may change the entire world. Everything starts with a thought, be it good or evil. Make the most of genuinely getting to know yourself and your thought process; it is a valuable audit.

Let us capture those thoughts, train those thoughts, never forgetting that in every single thought rests purpose.

Chapter 4

Stuck on Fear

"The things we fear the most may not cost us our lives but may rob us of many opportunities. In the end, the loss is inseparable." - **Ann- Monique Bailey Hutchinson**

Fear is much like glue, a glue that has no intention of easing up. It often clings without its host even acknowledging it, having grown so accustomed to its company. Fear can keep you as a prisoner, even when you have at your leisure many means of escape. It becomes an automatic response; the longer its damning hands are kept in your life. Experience has dictated that fear comes alive when possibilities and purpose announce their presence. Suppose an individual lives a life of purposelessness, aimlessly going through the days with no intention of changing this useless momentum. In that case, it is unlikely that he or she is bothered by anxiety or worry of any kind. While fear is attracted to intentionality, order, and decisiveness, it is also the enemy of these very things. It is ironic, but the fact is this, fear, much like living things, has its purpose, and that purpose seems to be the hindrance of our purpose.

Often, our fears become our reality with little effort, and when this happens, it stops us in our tracks. Many people struggle with the crippling effects of fear or will struggle with it at some point in their lives. Fear is not partial to color, class, shape, weight, or citizenship, but it does not just pop up. It is birthed in us through one medium or another, and when it is so birthed, it stays with those who often unwillingly invite it to do so. It is much like the uninvited guest who you want to leave your home, but you are ignorant about how to get him or her moving without confrontation. It makes you uncomfortable.

It usually causes a biochemical, emotional, or spiritual response that varies from individual to individual. The question is, why does it play such a massive role in this world, in our world? We live in a fallen world, but why can't we defeat fear more readily instead of the other way around? Yes, Lucifer comes to mind even as I type; no offence to any reader whose name might be Lucifer. However, if we are to blame the devil for our every action without taking responsibility for our role, we would never mature beyond a particular stage. The "devil made me do it" simply doesn't work forever. In addition to the enemy, other reasons could include but are not limited to:

- Instinct (It is natural and valuable but must not dominate)
- Past experiences, personally and otherwise
- Uncertainty about the future

- The possibility of disappointments
- Consequences, whether known or unknown
- Insecurities
- Anxiety
- People imposed opinions
- Ignorance (We fear what we do not know or understand)
- Expectations
- Our response to circumstances
- Control Issues (losing control)

This list is by no means comprehensive, but it is undoubtedly personal. In my life, one or a combination of these reasons has caused me to fear. It is worth considering the things that make us afraid. I did that to complete this list; I reviewed all the things that crippled my progress at some point.

I do not deny the usefulness of fear. It keeps us alert to danger at different points; it keeps us on our toes, informing us whether to lean towards our *flight or fight* instincts. The important thing is to know when to *"reign in"* that fear and when to play into it.

My husband can be quite philosophical, a trait I

welcome, as long as he does not use it against me. He dropped this bomb on me during one such moment, putting fear in a whole new light. He said quite calmly, "do not mistake fear for patience," unaware of the significance of his words to me. Initially, I could not understand the concept. He eventually explained, and when he did, I ultimately agreed. It is a mistake most of us have made, especially in our youth, when contemplating a big decision or the possibility of change. It is much one of those 'right time' kind of moments. In mistaking fear for patience, one disguises his or her fear beneath the cover of proceeding with caution or, worst, waiting patiently for *"the right time." "Let me wait and see first,"* you say. A moment of honesty here, however? Based on personal experience and after seeing others in the same boat, I know without a doubt, it is not always patience! It simply isn't. Instead, it is a close associate of it named fear. Waiting is vital in any circumstances, and yes, patience is critical, especially in Christians' lives. It is a fruit of the spirit, according to Galatians chapter 5.

Patience builds character in countless ways, and our failure to be patient may cause reckless decisions and life-changing consequences. I've learned that we must harness the ability to assess our motives and responses in varying circumstances. Without a doubt, we can be our own stumbling block when we fail to assess situations correctly. It is because fear can be such a game-changing emotion why we must act wisely and quickly. Not only does fear ultimately cripple forward movement, but it delays it too.

Delays can be as detrimental as a complete stop; it all depends on our perspective and the entire set of circumstances. We must learn that unless we move forward, fear wins. Unless we change our position, fear wins. These are words I would have forcefully shared with my younger self. I would have written myself this letter and insisted that I stopped waiting until the tides turned or on whatever I was waiting on or fearing.

It is not strange to imagine that someone who wants to get it all right would fear getting anything wrong true? And in trying to prevent this, it is almost inevitable that one cannot move beyond that place of fear. It becomes a barricade. It inhibits a breakthrough of knowledge and ideas. It is like an injured knee that temporarily rids you of your ability to walk. No longer can you walk into those blessings that God promised because of the fear of the fight the enemy also promises.

Fear of Failure

"Of all the liars in the world, sometimes the worst are our own fears." - Rudyard Kipling

Though useful in certain circumstances, fear can often be what I call the enemy of faith, almost the opposite of faith. It, unlike faith, anticipates great horrors, while without reason, true faith expects deliverance from terrors, seen and unseen. It inundates our sensibilities with gloomy prospects and cripples our ability to be truthful to ourselves and to those we have a hope of affecting.

Undoubtedly, I am acquainted with this liar named fear, but a crippling fear of failure further complicated this. The feeling of apprehension about getting things wrong prevented me from doing anything about so many things. On too many occasions, I decided that instead of failing, I would prefer not to engage in certain aspects of life. However, I have realized that we lose more due to our fears, real or imagined, than we do from reality by making fear an influencer. Even so, I have also learned that regrets change little but my moods and blood pressure.

My experience with fear has often been crippling. For several years, I learned the art of driving. I say art because, in Jamaica, it honestly seems that way. When I was younger, two of my uncles, a cousin, and my grandfather gave me driving lessons. When I was seventeen years old, another associate allowed me to drive his car when I went overseas for the first time—insane, right? My youngest brother, Adrian, and my now husband, Leroy, were the ones who eventually helped me to conquer some of my fears. My husband was in a more consistent position to teach me. So he had to endure the fearful blunders I made during the training process. He knows well how my fears delayed me from obtaining my license. I received my second provisional license when I was about Twenty-Five years old. I worked as an Attorney-at-Law in Morant Bay, St. Thomas.

What did I fear? Failing the test for one and crashing one of my then *'significant other's* (now husband) vehicle was the other. I was not too fond of being told that I was not a good driver if I failed the test. Admittedly, I was not the best driver in training, and I disliked not being good at it. I figured driving would be as simple as it looked when I sat in a motor vehicle's front passenger seat 'driving' for the actual driver. What a rude awakening those driving lessons were.

But the fear of failure held me back long enough and eventually almost caused me to fail the actual test.

Thankfully, I succeeded the first time around, a feat I managed while dealing with dengue fever-like symptoms. This small victory was several months after I purchased my car—what a journey it was and what a sky-high insurance package too! In the end, I did not mind too much. It was worth the sacrifice. Before I got my license, I can recall one instance where my former landlady told me she wanted to do her lawn. She asked me to move the car. Perhaps I could start it, but I could not drive it. I was angry at myself, at her, but I had no one to blame but myself and my fears—unfounded fears at that. Fear stops not only you from doing things; it also prevents you from evening knowing you can do the deed. It wipes away both the reality and the possibility; that is how powerful fear can be. It can survive in your past, present, and future, all because of your present worries. Our fears give fear a superpower and rob us of our superpower of being fearfully and wonderfully made.

Fear keeps you up at night and startle you awake in the earliest of mornings. It goes as far as you allow it. Feed your fear, and it becomes you. Starve it, and it eventually vacates your mind, body, and soul. I had to learn this, slowly but yes, it made all the difference. Now, just over a year after getting my license, I have driven to every parish in Jamaica by myself except for Portland, both early mornings and late nights. I enjoy driving so much now; I might consider speed racing. Don't tell my parents I said that.

Fear is binding; being free of it is the most enlightening feeling one can feel, especially after being held captive by it for so long. No one should have to experience such crippling emotions, it is not of God, and it is not healthy. So once more, I encourage myself, I encourage you, heal.

The 'Enemies' of Success

In his motivational presentations, Steve Harvey would often remind his audience that success requires arduous work and sacrifice. While I agree with Mr. Harvey, I believe that these two requirements and success are subjective. Why would I say this? Well, realistically, what I consider successful and valuable may be of no moment to others. Values and goals will vary from individual to individual, and so will their responses to your success. It is, therefore, vital that one's sense of self is highly developed, all the while resisting the pressure to impose unrealistic expectations on you.

Oh, the pressure! Balance is once more at the forefront of the list of must-haves in the life of one keen on overcoming the need to be perfect or, better yet, to appear perfect. I find that once I strike this delicate balance, then whether someone claps for me, cheer me on, or otherwise recognizes my progress, it matters nil! Congratulate yourself, celebrate yourself and raise praises to God almighty because you worked hard for that milestone, whatever it may be. That blessing was given to you and will remain except at the will of God. You better recognize the hurdle crossed. More than all, remember you are entitled to celebrate and feel ecstatic about it!

This is the perfect picture painted above, the image of how it should be, but nothing will ever be exactly as it should be until the Lord returns. *"If only that would sink in and stay in all the time,"* is what I said to myself as I typed this very paragraph. This is my mindset at this stage of life, but it has not always been that way. Either way, it is the best-case scenario because we like to be appreciated, complimented, and congratulated as humans. Some of us have high up on our love language ladder, words of affirmation.

For those who care about the response they get when they share their joys, I can undoubtedly say they are watching both words and actions. I can recall saying to a few people on more than occasion that actions speak way louder than words. However, this is not necessarily the case with others who appreciate kind words or, as Gary Chapman puts it, words of affirmation. Let's take the romance out of it and apply it to humans in general. Here, **words** are everything. Whether they are written or spoken, a person who shares her successes with another expects a response. Therefore, she places some importance on what you have to say to her. Perhaps expectations are the problem. If so, I would recommend that she reduces her expectations so disappointments are not induced.

Whether we like it or not, we all have certain built-in expectations. To ask otherwise of a person who has worked hard to get to a particular stage or level would with the normal man be unfair. The reality does not change that not everyone will celebrate our highs. Yes, it might be a little hard to swallow. However, along life's road, we may all have to deal with people who cannot celebrate you. However, we cannot be so fearful of offending people or being shunned by them that we fear sharing with others and testifying about the goodness of the Lord. If it ever gets that bad, then perhaps it is full-time we confront ourselves about our hang-ups. Maybe we need to accept that not everyone will celebrate with you or should celebrate with you.

Fear insistently complains, worries, and hesitates. It holds you back from sharing the part of yourself that you worked hard on and which you also believe to be perfect enough, not perfect, but enough, to share with the rest of the world.

Sometimes, I appreciate my tendency to pause before sharing things. This is simply because some victories are not for the public eye. I have also realized that sharing your success may cause the recipient of the good news to stumble further into bitterness, envy, malice and negative emotions continue. This dear, if it should happen, is not on you but is instead a symbol of that person's maturity or lack thereof. Questions of *"why did I tell him or her, why did I post it, vlogged about it, or blogged about it"* may play around in your head for a second.

Again, as I came to acknowledge, this is not a *"my*

problem" moment. I still remind myself that moments like these allow me to point a finger in the opposite direction and say, *"this is on you, hunae!"* I freely admit then that not everything is about me, that the world does not revolve around me! If someone you trusted enough to share your wins with chooses not to celebrate you, well then, life does not pack up and leave. It continues!

Therefore, it is imperative to balance the scales of sharing; this becomes a part of the network of issues. If one is not careful, anxiety may pop up and throw the entire system out of whack.

We will have *'mis-takes'* along the way to becoming a better version of ourselves. Still, we should not throw tantrums when our destination is unexpected or unwanted. Instead, we innovate, and we try to make the best of the circumstances if, for no other reason, but to ensure that we learn, grow, and finish strong at the end of that journey.

Chapter 5

Angry Birdie

"Fools give full vent to their rage, but the wise bring calm in the end." **Proverbs 29: 11 (N.I.V.)**

Even Samuel didn't get it right the first time around. If only a perfectionist would understand that sometimes, we do not get it right the first time and usually not even the second or third time. I do believe this is the one thing I struggled with the most, and even now, I have to remind myself that the only being who gets it right all the time is God! Yes, we are made in his image. Yes, I am a big fan of the oldie but goodie, the hymn, *"To be like Jesus, to be like Him..."* but we are all human and therefore affected by the human condition. And so, which Samuel are you talking about, Ann- Monique? Relax, darlings; I'm getting to him. Old Samuel, one of the GOAT (*Greatest of All Times*) prophets, was born in 1 Samuel 1: 20, in answer to Hannah's prayer. In 1 Samuel 3: 4-10, we read where the Lord called Samuel all of three times before he finally came to realize that Eli was not calling him, but instead, the Lord!

What an incredible call! Still, he messed up thrice before finally understanding that he was being called by someone far more extraordinary than Eli or anyone he would ever know. Had he missed this call, he would have missed a lot; he would have missed out on hearing and heeding the call of the Lord upon his life.

What was interesting was his response or lack thereof in the mind of some. In his innocence, Samuel was as cool as a cucumber!

Sometimes, innocence shrouds us from the turmoil of negative emotions, allowing us to accept outward instructions more readily. He wisely sought help from Eli because he knew Eli was more knowledgeable than he was. He trusted Eli's guidance. Suppose he was more exposed, hardened by the disappointments of life, by people calling him only to waste his time. In that case, his response to the call and his mistake may have been a little different. Samuel eventually realized what he could have missed out on, but it did not negatively affect his actions.

How many of us beat ourselves up about what we almost missed out on, about what we would have started earlier? How many of us said if only I had learned this lesson a little sooner, I could have been further along? This is despite not 'missing out,' just almost missing out, and despite starting, even though one started later than you could have.

The *"if only(s)"* in our lives have caused much-misguided anger. *"If only"* we knew this before; perhaps we could better process the variety of things in life that continue to provoke us to wrath.

The Inside You

While watching *Iron Man 2*, I witnessed the deterioration of Tony Stark's behavior publicly and with those he loved. Yes, he had a bad attitude from the very beginning; his character was arrogant, selfish, and immature. One would think it could not get any worst for him, but it did. He distanced himself from those he could rely on, publicly embarrassed himself, and lost his precious iron man suit. He then drank himself into stupid situations and hurt the woman he loved because his inside was breaking down. Physically, he was dying; poison was coursing through his blood. His mind was broken, and his spirit was broken. This was what was on the inside of Tony Stark, and sure as could be, it came out externally. He was an angry bomb waiting to explode.

Even as I think about the film, the truth of the circumstances continues to hit hard. When we are not okay on the inside, we show it on the outside. Who we are inside will show outside for as long as we leave these issues untended. However, we need not give in to those feelings. It takes time, it takes patience, and it takes commitment. Biting our tongues until we heal is hard; picking up the pieces after yielding to an angry fit is hard. Choose your hard. So how do we not cave to the negativity that keeps on spurring us? From my experience, these tips below are worthwhile:

- *He had to seek help.* This step is one of the hardest for people who become so self-reliant and gets used to doing things to their level of so-called perfection. But there are some things we cannot solve by ourselves because we are not experts in life; no one is, except God himself. When he did so, the person came up with a solution that saved his life and did the second thing we often need in these cases, healed him.

- *Heal!* This is a process; it can be more painful than the hurts itself, but it is worth it. Walking around with toxic mess within is not only painfully dangerous to the carrier, but it also releases poisonous emotional messes on those around us. We all want to maintain a sense of privacy about our lives (*for those who are not social media influencers or otherwise public persons*). Know this, though; the more persons we allow to see our anger and other negative emotions, the more we expose the most bruised, battered, and private parts of ourselves. Heal, it is worth it.

- *Change your perspective.* Focus on what you can do to change the situation and not the person who made you angry. The latter will never happen, but the former, it is all in your hands and the hands of the almighty himself. Well, God can change the person, but if we want to admit it, often we are angry for all the wrong reasons and sometimes, even at the wrong person. A change in our perspective can change our entire mood and mindset and reduce the anger we feel.

- Without a doubt, anger is often seen through the carrier's eyes; naturally, it will see life through different eyes. It is as if one eye is covered; that is the eye of reason, understanding, and patience, and you see life only through the eyes of your pain, your hurt, and your needs. Anger quickly becomes a very selfish emotion, and everything becomes about you only. I have only been able to release the anger successfully when I pause long enough to allow another perspective to come into my line of thoughts. I have to look at things differently, change my train of thought and do so while maintaining personal standards. Changing your perspective does not mean letting go of your values and ideals, just that you consider other people's own too. Albert Einstein said it firmly, *"we cannot solve our problems with the same thinking we used when we created them."*

- ***Self-Answering:*** "A s*oft answer turneth away wrath but grievous words, stir up anger." (Proverbs 15:1KJV)* The word of God forever produces antidotes to the harshest of conditions. We generally associate this with how we respond to other people but rarely do we assess how we address ourselves, especially when displeased with our actions or inactions. I have been guilty of cursing myself out for messing up, genuinely digging in, creating self-inflicted emotional wounds that eventually caused bruises for others nearby. It takes practice to make this change, but this change is necessary when you no longer want to be a ticking time bomb waiting to explode. The way we speak to ourselves at our lowest points can make all the difference to us. You matter! If you can regulate how you talk to others, why not do the very same for yourself?

- **Let not the sun go down on your anger.** (Ephesians 4:26 K.J.V.) This command is relatively simple. Let it go! Quickly!

No Cheerleaders?

When you do what you love, and you're doing well

at what you love, it is a warm and precious feeling to hear someone say, "Well done." The reality is, no matter how well you do or how much you have grown, not everyone will notice. Not everyone will say well done, and not everyone will consider it a big deal. Should it matter? Based on our love language, we may care, especially if words of affirmation give you the thrills and make you feel all warm and tingly. If not, then who cares, right? Some care, maybe too much.

I have been there and migrated from there. It is a burdensome place to live, the *land of waiting on someone to pat you on the back and tell you a fantastic job*. When it does not happen, and you get criticism or silence instead, 'oh man,' the slap across the face. It feels somewhat like preparing for a major speech and walking instead into an empty auditorium. Heartbreaking.

Then comes growth and the decision to do what you do and not care one bit about who wants to cheer you on or run you out! It is one of the most amazing and freeing places to be. To win and celebrate in private, to create history, albeit in smaller circles, and celebrate without waiting on anyone to say "congrats!" There is nothing like doing something well and speaking to yourself, *"that's an innovative idea; I like it."* Sometimes, it is good to toot your own horn. There would be little need to become angry at people who do not call or text with celebratory messages and comments.

Yes, one must stick with people who will rejoice for you, people who will share genuinely in your journey, but when these people do not exist, life must still go on. The show must always go on. We have to become our own and favorite cheerleaders if we are to survive emotionally and physically in this increasingly selfish world.

As humans, we are almost innately selfish, and so the first thought in most of our minds is *"me,"* not others, not you, not us, just *"me."* To grow beyond people-pleasing for the sake of applause or promotion, we must realize that some things must only be about us. Not in an egotistical sense, no but to the extent that we must be our own most exceptional support system except for God. Everyone around you is fallible, and so are you. Still, at least, you get to know yourself first. In that process, tell yourself how imperative it is to be there for you and how key it is to be your own biggest cheerleader, even in public silence.

Many of us can relate to each other's struggles and

weaknesses far better than we realize because we, too, have the same issues. Life would be an easier battle to fight if we admitted that and desist from holding others to our standards. Life is not only visible through your eyes or my eyes. Over Seven Billion other eyes are looking at life too, so we must, therefore, remember, perspective is fundamental!

A little birdie once said the following:
- Sometimes, silence is a mighty weapon, more powerful than any automatic weapon or reactions or words of anger.
- Sometimes, anger is control issues parading itself as anger.
- Sometimes, anger is also selfishness.

Chapter 6

Outside In

"It's not what happens to you; it's what happens in you. You don't have control of outward circumstances, but you do have control of your inward attitudes." **John Maxwell**

Whenever I am sending a text message, my face generally reflects what I am typing. During the summer of 2020, I can recall breaking down emotionally after a rough day. A message came in from a friend who needed some encouragement. That was the last thing I wanted to do. I wanted to mope, get annoyed at someone, feel sorry for myself, you know, the usual list of things one experiences on days like those.

I had a choice to make, and so, after spilling a few more tears and flipping the phone on its face to avoid confronting that person's needs, I took it up the said phone and typed. What left my fingers were kind words of encouragement I so badly wanted to hear at the moment. That started a shift within, unknown to me just then. As I typed, I took a while to realize that though the tears were still flowing, I was smiling. My inside voice was pushing out positivity and tears all at once, but the smile was coming forth. By the time I was through with the text, my tears were no more, and the fog and tension in my mind were clearing up.

Often, our insides do not match what the world is fortunate to observe on the outside. Many people perfect the 'art' of wearing a 'mask' so well. When wearing masks became mandatory in certain countries in 2020, the physical mask felt like a disguise over what had become their accepted mask of falsehood. I dare to say that if one begins and continues to wear superman's or batman's costume twenty-four hours every day for years, eventually, you might feel tempted to fly off tall buildings, peer through walls and capture bad guys in one 'Gotham' or the other.

I have proven that when you attempt to be someone you are not, even if with the right motivation, discovering who you are will become that much harder. Without pretenses, this search is tedious. When you add pretending to the mix and the need to heal from the tendency to act, a dangerously steep road is ahead. I mentioned in previous chapters that while healing is necessary, it can be painful, especially after pretending to be who you aren't for so long. Eventually, we look like what we pretend to be and, and we lose ourselves completely. Our insides no longer reflect what is on the outside.

Nothing is more debilitating to a person's emotional and personal development than pretending to be someone he/she is not. Often, the pretense is not merely to be or do something but instead to be or do something so someone else can believe that you have it all together. Show me the person with it altogether, and you'll be showing me God or Christ Jesus himself. Only they have it all together.

The question of whether our 'outside' reflects our 'inside' continues to force introspection. Only an honest and mature person will pause and consider the subject. After that, only a person wishing to grow will make adjustments upon figuring out that what the world sees of her, what she shows, is truly not what is happening on the inside. Whatever is there may not be helpful, but at least this admission could allow one to begin the healing process. This was the mirror I had to look into on my journey. Do our outsides reflect what is going on inside us, or are we wearing masks? How well are we wearing the masks, or are the masks wearing us?

The 'Root' of the Matter Is

Everything that we become has its roots in our past actions or actions done to us in the past. Now, the Bible does encourage us to *"forget those things which are behind"* and press towards the future, which holds things of higher importance. However, before we relocate to our new homes in glory, we must assess our current state of being and determine whether there is anything within which is worth changing. I guarantee that unless you believe yourself *"to have already attained,"* then you will find there are dysfunctional *'twigs'* in our lives that need adjustment. There are things in our past that some of us can never mention publicly because of the new can of worms it might open. There are those things that, while they may not be so drastic, they have left a mark on our current state of being and will undeniably affect our future. These things are the root of every new issue, I believe. Our past can either make us who we are, and we stay that way, or we can acknowledge our history, heal accordingly and then become better. The latter is much more challenging but far more valuable.

Many of us are guilty of adopting bad habits and making poor decisions, and so we cannot blame everything on our past. We must, however, be mindful of those things closely connected. I was listening to a snippet of a Joyce Meyer teaching recently. She spoke about what individuals could adjust to avoid wasting time. She started by encouraging her audience to get rest. She pulled out all the things that could result from failing to do so. Joyce showed how all things start somewhere and are connected. She moved from lack of rest to anger issues and edginess that could arise from this lack of rest.

As I contemplated her scenarios, an expanded picture was painted in my mind, an image of negative possibilities that could be bred from a simple situation. Take a ride with me and say, for example, you fail to get enough rest one weeknight and maintain this habit for a few weeks because of work and personal habits. In the mornings, you drag yourself out of bed and rush off to go to work. On the way to work, you have several near misses on the roads because, let us be honest; you are tired! Focusing is next to impossible!

Tension rises in your head as you drive; drivers are not operating well, nor are the pedestrians using the road well, adding to your frustration. Increasingly, you become annoyed at all the road users. When you finally get to work, at least half-hour late, you barely speak to your colleagues. Who knows, you may even explode on your boss and then think that might cost you a promotion or, worst, your job! You become edgier, even as your relationships break down. Your job suffers, your peace is lost, and you cannot sleep at night with the marathon of thoughts confronting you when you lay your head to rest.

To find comfort, you start to stress-eat, and naturally, you gain weight, and people notice. The not-so-sensitive people see the gain and pass offensive remarks. You are now tired, tense, and angry. You are underperforming at work, about you lose your job, overweight, and addicted to food, low on self-esteem, socially and emotionally distant, and life looks terrible. You consider, is it all worth it? A scenario like this is the reality for many people who we may not know. Without a doubt, everything is connected.

It started from a lack of healthy sleeping habits and went downhill to considering whether life itself was worth it. Failing to take care of one area of our life can cause dreadful consequences for many or all other areas. I can attest to the edginess resulting from a lack of sleep. I have experienced the anxiety that fast-approaching deadlines may cause. Then there is the temperament after driving on Jamaican roads for just about a year and a half now! A life-changing experience, I tell you! There is something about driving on our streets, whatever the parish might be, that causes you to question your salvation and, sometimes, your sanity. It can drive an insane person sane and a sane person over the walls, but that is an issue for another time.

Thankfully, I have engaged in working on these areas of my life, but I had to ponder this one question, when did it all start? Unless one gets to the root of the issues that continually pop up, you will fall like a tree with diseased roots. We are intelligent people; we know that trees cannot come back to life. The good thing is, we can! Physically and emotionally, and spiritually! What a mighty God we serve!

The caveat is, this will only happen if one is interested in getting that inside you into the right shape. This transformation takes time, it takes commitment, and it takes honesty. It may also require some counseling, which I have no significant issue with, especially having gone through it individually and while preparing for marriage. We don't have all the answers, and that is fine.

Sometimes, we must take everything apart, and sometimes, we'll need help to smash the walls of our past into nothingness and recreate something beautiful. Similarly, in the *HGTV* series, *Good Bones*, we see most of the dilapidated structures eventually broken into bits by the show's hosts and laborers. The structure's functional portions often remain standing as the foundation for the rebuilding of something great. Sometimes, we must destroy the facade we have going on in our minds before we can see the colossal mess we cover so well with external deflectors.

Mostly, we cannot view the root of the tree in its fullness until we dig way below the surfaces where we will get our hands dirty; see some creepy crawlies, broken leaves, broken glass, stones, and more. In digging, the glass may cut us, and so can the rocks. The creepy crawlers will scare us, but we must get to the root. Such is the way to healing, a beautiful, painful reality.

"It Wasn't Me."

Orville Richard Burrell, better known by his stage name, 'Shaggy,' has recorded numerous hit songs since the start of his musical career in the 1990s. In the year 2000, a year after Virgin Music dropped him, he signed with DreamWorks and released the Album *"Hot Shot,"* which featured the smash hit song, *"It Wasn't Me."* The song made the rounds, topping the Billboard Hot 100 and reaching number one in the

United Kingdom, Ireland, Scotland, France, and other countries. It was one of the most popular songs in the 2000s while I was in primary (grade) school, and to date, it remains one of his most popular hits.

While the song was such a hit, its title is far more applicable to real-life than many think. In reality, we all have to deal with the ever-present battle of accepting responsibility for our actions and our inactions. We have to balance also, knowing when to take on responsibility and when to leave it be for the right person to claim it.

In my journey of growth, there was an overwhelming struggle with taking on too much responsibility for something or failing to take on enough. The things I have blamed myself for would shock even the people involved in the situations. Two such instances which stand out include a childhood friend's death by suicide and a close friend and relative's pregnancy when she was twenty years old. Mind you; at the time of one of these occurrences, I was not even living in Jamaica; I was studying and living in Husband Gardens, Barbados.

I can recall the day my cousin called and told me she was pregnant. I cried, and so did she. I was angry at myself for not being in Jamaica by her side, motivating her to finish strong with her personal and educational goals. I was consumed with guilt for not being a physically present leader. I told myself that had I stayed in Jamaica to study or not go to college at all; I could have been a better youth leader, a better cousin to her. No, it wasn't so much the pregnancy itself, but what it meant for my cousin then; that some dreams would have to be put on hold, some permanently, some indefinitely. Yes, crazy, I know, but as I said before, it was a struggle. I beat myself stupid for what had little to do with me. Her pregnancy had nothing to do with me at all! (*Update! Today she is all grown and happily married!*) To think that I spent ages blaming myself for the journey choices of a grown woman! I quickly learned that it wasn't always about me, even if what I wanted was the best for the person. Everyone has to make his or her own choices and, after that, live with the consequences.

My struggles with blame became a little more challenging when someone I knew from my childhood days died by suicide. After hearing about the death, I asked myself a question, *"what if I had been there? Would I have been able to help the situation, perhaps offer some unofficial counselling?"* Quickly, I took on to myself a giant pillow of guilt, for reasons only God knows. Yes, I know that everything is not all about me, and it does sound strange now that I think about it.

However, I was trying to balance studying in another country while maintaining my role as a Youth Leader. I didn't understand then that I should wisely choose my battles. Perhaps it was the guilt of choosing my studies in another country, automatically putting ministry on the 'backburner.' I didn't want to make choices that benefitted me only. I did not understand then, as intelligent as I was, that people's decisions were not reflections of who I was.

As a Youth Leader who was building a good relationship with youths in my then local church and my immediate environs, I wanted to change lives. I wanted everyone to become his or her best self right then. I was selfishly thinking I could 'help' everyone become what they wanted to be, and when things didn't go how *I* thought they should in the time it should, I pointed the finger at one person; *me*. Yes, I know, crazy. It had nothing to do with ego then, but perhaps I would diagnose myself with a god-complex if I did the same thing now. We thank God for growth and maturity.

Lessons from the Outside
From that period of my life, I have since learned many lessons, the greatest of them being, not everything is about me, and not everything is my fault. We can want the best for others, but everyone is responsible for their successes and failures.

Failures are not something I have always accepted as necessary, as my fault, or sometimes, as existing. Sometimes I took on too much. At other times, I was often in denial about things not working out, primarily because of something I either did or did not do. If you always want things to go right, when they go wrong, and trust me, many things will go wrong, admitting that you caused it to be so is not always easy. I think it gets more challenging when you know there can be apparent consequences for your failure from God, parents, teachers, or employers. Finding someone to cast the blame is easy until you get older and hopefully wiser. Then, you realize you never learned all you should have.

Now, I am learning to value and admit to failures. I make an effort to accept failure as an opportunity to understand that we are flawed, complicated, imperfect humans, and not little gods. While losses are difficult to accept, real growth demands taking responsibility for necessary things and circumstances, controlling our actions, inactions, and reactions. If and only if we do this, will change become possible, a necessary change that is. From this change can be birthed a new mindset of becoming a better version of ourselves.

Chapter 7

Likes, Views, Comments!

"Life is the most difficult exam of all. Many people fail because they try to copy others, not realizing everyone is answering different questions"- **Dale Partridge**

As a student, going through the ropes of Basic, Primary, and High school, I recall being presented with various essay topics to give my touch of expertise to (Laughs). More than once, teachers gave me essays with the subject *"Who Is Your Role Model?"* or a variation of the question when I was younger. I would usually write about two persons, including my mother, Marlene E. Bailey, whom I love dearly. I saw her examples as worth following in most cases. To date, I still do. I do not believe she is perfect, but she is an exemplary woman who strives to be a great representation of a balanced human. As I read new books and watched more television series, my delicate mind entered a world where my space was continuously filled with outside and strange influences. It became a task to ignore what was around me, not to allow it to influence who I was and who I wanted to be. I was a child, and that is when you are often made or broken.

Life did not break me, but for those who know me exceptionally well, for example, my parents, my husband, and my youngest of three brothers, I had enough reason to have been broken. Thankfully, I learned how to be strong, reasonably early, and have lovely parents and a reliable support system.

While my parents raised me to be independent, intelligent, and good, I have gone through moments where I was guilty of trying to be like someone else. For me, it was primarily like characters in novels I read from primary school to my late teens. At one point, I wanted to be a Detective with the Federal Bureau of Investigations because Nancy Drew was a cool chick detective, and I wanted to go one better. Eventually, I met up on Alex Cross in the James Patterson series of books. I now wanted to be a detective and an Attorney-at-Law, and possibly a Teacher. Those are just the tip of the iceberg, but you get the gist. I eventually chose what I wanted to do professionally with the help of God. There were detours before I got there, much like everyone else on their way to becoming their best self.

I will always support individuals running their own race. No one will face the exact obstacles you face. No one will have the same parents you do, no one will be blessed the exact way you are, and with these differences, how could it be that we want to attain the same prizes others get at the end of their races? Some people are running a race *for* their lives, and that's just one race, while others are merely running *one of* the many races they will need to win to get to where they should be. We cannot know everyone's story, and as such, we should not envy or wish to be the star of anyone's show. Cliché, but *run your own race*.

Versus (Competition)

I mentioned earlier that I have been writing for almost two decades. Unfortunately, I have published none of those books beyond the popular online platform, Wattpad. The decision not to publish in my latter years was to some extent because I saw numerous persons 'dropping' books all over. It no longer felt original. Ironically, I almost felt like others were telling my story before I got to do so, and it was heartbreaking. Silly me, now that I think about it. Only you can tell your story, any part or portion of it you so desire.

Fortunately, my husband wisely reminded me that before I became an Attorney-at-Law, there were thousands of Lawyers across the world, but still, I followed the same career path. Simply put but very accurate. The lesson learned was that I could not allow another person's journey to stop me. Additionally, I could not let it force me to begin a journey God did not call me to start. I now understand that I must be mindful of when to ignore influence.

If we can see others who have finished their race before we even begin ours or while we were running our journey, we should use what we have sight of to motivate our own internal and developmental race.

We cannot allow them to cause us to stumble or otherwise feel as if we have lost the race of life. Is it only about winning? We are already involved in an eternal race with the enemy of our souls, Satan. This race will continue to the end of our life here on this earth. We want to win this race, but it is not all about winning with our fellow humans. You have stopped your race before you even started once you decide that it is about winning and not about running. When your race becomes about running and running your 'own' race, it is easy for you to accept that along with running, starting becomes the next best thing.

After that, continuing, learning, and never giving up becomes critical. Even when it looks like and people may be saying you are losing, you know your race. Stay confidently running, always remembering that it is not all about winning.

Life is the only race that does not have solely one winner. We can all get a gold medal in this race, so long as we finish well. Use the other runners around you as mentors but never an adverse competition. The real battle should be between you and who you *could* become if you do and be what and who you are called to become.

Likes and Views

And while we are busy doing what we know God called us to do, we ought to be caught up with whether God likes it and views it as a part of his good and perfect will, not the likes and views of those in the world we live. Have you ever wondered, *"what if they don't approve? What if they don't like it or me?"* I have, and what did that earn me? Anxiety issues, desiring to do everything so well and still messing up everything because I focused on the wrong thing...likes!

Jamaican Reggae artiste Jamar Rolando McNaughton, also called Chronixx, said it best in his hit song *'Likes.'* He sang beautifully, *"Dweet fi di love, me nuh dweet fi di likes."* He was declaring that whatever he did, he did it for the love of it, not to garner likes from external sources. That mindset breeds many things, one of which is PEACE! What a blissful feeling to be living your life with no care in the world about who might like it, so long as you are not doing anything unlawful and immoral.

For my purposes, immoral speaks to behavior that does not conform to accepted standards, the highest standards being those outlined in the word of God.

Imagine the conditions of our hearts if we adjusted our motives to line up with God's words, good morals, and sound wisdom, instead of solely to obtain clicks, likes, views, and positive comments? What would we lose if we did more for the views of God? Nothing. How much better would we see ourselves, more so through His eyes and not the eyes of the world? To do this, we have first to adjust our views of ourselves, our view of God and become more familiar with how God views us.

The standard by which we live should properly be how *God* sees us, not how others view us or whether they like us and what we represent. The latter mindset will drain every bit of who you are, leaving behind a sad shell of what the world prefers you to be. Trust me when I say that such a mental and emotional space is a terrible place to be in. Even though God never leaves us nor forsakes us, the world offers no such comfort. We live in a fallen and selfish world, and therefore, we cannot expect perfection from each other.

We often question the lack of applause when we do something we think was well done. Many remain silent while boldly monitoring our every move, great moves, and those moves we eventually regret making. In those cases, some mean you well by not saying anything and refraining from saying whether they like or dislike the action, inaction, or statement.

Not everything we put out there ought to be out there for others to see—some things we need to keep between God and us. Keeping our mouths and fingers from oversharing becomes a little bit easier when we do less for likes and views and more for God's approval.

We know that evil exists, but I understand now more than ever that while some people are wicked other people are weak. Sometimes, things happen to us at their hands, not because they are evil but because they had a moment of weakness.

This reality is even more reason not to put our trust in people. Not to rely on the views, likes, or dislikes of another, but to build ourselves up so much that ultimately, we get to the place where only God's opinion matters.

Comments

Words by themselves are inherently powerful. When we activate words by speaking them to or over someone's life, they become engines of success or brakes of depression, anger, and pain so deep that many struggle to survive them. Author Carlos Ruiz Zafón had several insightful moments in his book *'The Shadow of the Wind.'* He asserted that *"the words, with which a child's heart is poisoned, whether through malice or ignorance, remain branded in his memory, and sooner or later they burn his soul."*

So yes, Zafón addressed the damaging effects of words on children solely. Still, it would not be difficult to attribute the same results to an adult in a similar set of circumstances. Words are not partial to age. My past experiences have shown me that the more delicate your state of mind, emotions, and level of maturity, the more vulnerable you are to external verbal attacks.

Amanda Todd's story has been glued to my mind ever since I first heard it while watching a series named *"Web of Lies"* on ID television. She was a 15 years old Canadian teenager who felt the brunt of hundreds of comments from persons known and unknown to her. She felt the words so much that life for her became a painful burden. On September 7, 2012, Amanda posted a video called *"My story: Struggling, bullying, suicide, self-harm"* on YouTube. A month and five days later, on October 12, 2012, she was found dead in her hometown of Port Coquitlam, British Columbia. She, unfortunately, took her own life, only a few hours after she told her mother she was well.

"Hello, I've decided to tell you about my never-ending story," the black and white video began. Amanda Todd could only be seen from her nose down for most of the video. She silently told her story through white cards with the words inked in black on them. She described using online chats to meet and talk to new people as a seventh-grade student. During conversations on these chats, people told her she was "stunning, beautiful, and perfect." On one such occasion, a strange man pressured her to show her breasts, and one year later, she yielded to his demand. Shortly after, she received a message on Facebook from another man who threatened to distribute the photo of her chest to everyone if she failed to *"put on a show"* for him.

Over the Christmas holiday, the police came to her house and confirmed her worst fears. Someone sent the photo to everyone. This sparked her struggles with anxiety, depression, and panic disorders. Her entire life changed. She quickly became the headline of everyone's conversation on social media, and the world saw it all. This forced her mother to relocate, and soon, she started to do drugs and drink alcohol.

A year after moving, Amanda thought things were back to normal. Unfortunately, the man on Facebook came back, and the photo of her chest was his new display picture. Amanda said she *"cried every night, lost all my friends and respect people had for me again. I can never get that photo back... it's out there forever."*

She was called names, she felt ignored, and eventually, she began to cut herself. She stated that she made a *"huge mistake"* and *"hooked up"* with a boy at her school who already had a girlfriend. A week later, persons sent her text messages, demanding that she quit school. Later, a group of her schoolmates, led by the boy's girlfriend, surrounded her on the school compound.

One guy then yelled, *"Just punch her already,"* so the girlfriend did just that.

Amanda wrote in the video on one of the cards, *"She threw me to the ground and punched me several times. Kids filmed it. I was all alone and left on the ground."*

She stated that she *"wanted to die so"* badly. Her father found her in a ditch that day. Her torture did not stop there. She had to be rushed to the hospital to have her stomach pumped after drinking bleach when she went home that said day. After she arrived home, she saw that strangers had plastered her Facebook timeline with cruel comments such as *"She deserved it. I hope she's dead."*

Amanda relocated once again to another school in another city, but the social media torture persisted. Students coldly suggested that she tried another bleach and shared photographs of ditches.

She asked as the video ended, *"Every day, I think, why am I still here? I'm stuck. What's left of me now? Nothing stops. I have nobody. I need someone. My name is Amanda Todd."*

On October 10, 2012, the police drove to a residence in Port Coquitlam, British Columbia, to investigate the tortured teenager's unexpected death. She was in the tenth grade at the Coquitlam Alternate Basic Education School when she died.

We have a choice in this life, no matter the circumstances. Admittedly, it is far easier to take the option out of our own hands and lay the blame at the feet of a tight situation, limited time, financial struggles, and the actions of others. Most of us like comfort and ease. In these circumstances, Todd's choice to end her life was heavily and unfortunately affected by the decisions of selfish, cruel, and sociopathic persons.

While I wish she had made another choice, and while I do not support suicide, I believe some of us have been where it seemed like there is no other choice but to quit fighting and stop living. When you add hurtful, unsupportive, emotionally disruptive comments to the mix, these often become the push we truly never needed, pushing some beyond the edge.

I have realized and accepted that words have hands that can reach beyond borders, beyond oceans, beyond climate and time zones. They are much like limitless weapons of mass destruction or like inquisitive engineers with the ability to either build or destroy. Words can give life, and words can take life. Words can mend, and words can break. The bible says in Proverbs 18:21, *"Death and life are in the power of the tongue: and they that love it shall eat the fruit thereof."* Clearer words than this one cannot find! While many live to break others with their words and comments, there are those whose lives depend on whether anyone comments or gives feedback.

Many of us still find it challenging to grasp this concept. We have victimized others with our words, been a victim of the words of others or made ourselves victims by seeking the comments and feedback from others who really and truly could not care less about your well-being. My parents raised me to understand the value of words quickly, but yes, sometimes I miss the point.

Many speak in ignorance, failing utterly to understand the lasting scars that their spoken or written words have on their intended recipient. When that recipient already struggles with who she is, where she is, and why she is, try to imagine how much more complicated things become, primarily when the words are spoken by people she values or otherwise aspires to be like in one way or the other. While I advocate for individuality, we cannot deny that sometimes, we struggle with ourselves in our lives. Some of us often wish we were elsewhere, being someone else, doing something else, and living someone else's dreams. Good for you if you've never been there and good for me, I have moved on from there.

Some may survive the phase and the cruel comments; others will wish themselves away from the pain of it all. It depends on the circumstances of each case. Adult 'me' would not respond to some things the way teenage 'me' did, and if I did, I would be worried. So we have to be mindful that we don't attack others, especially when we do not know their mindset and the stage of life they are at emotionally. We must be mindful not to defend our imperfections and bathe them with the falsity of perfection; we do not wish to stunt another person's development. Words give life, and it takes away.

Chapter 8

Third-Party Rights

"Life is 10% what happens to me and 90% of how I react to it." – **John Maxwell**

Surprise! A legal-sounding turn is this? That may not surprise many, especially for those who know that by profession, I am an Attorney-at-Law. I've written quite a few unpublished novels where the heroine is an Attorney-at-Law or a law student. Law always seems to fall into the mix of things naturally, and I simply let it flow.

In law, third-party rights would naturally pop up in discussions about contractual agreements. It arose based on the doctrine of privity. In simple terms, this doctrine says that unless you are party to the contract, that is, the promise or the promisor, you have no right to sue based on the contract. Additionally, you do not have any obligations under the contract, as a general rule. You may benefit from the agreement, but there can be no imposition of liability.

As in most legal situations, there are exceptions to this rule. If you do not fall under one exception, then the egg is on your face, whether or not the contract was made for your benefit. The exceptions include but are not limited to:

1. Statutory Exceptions
2. Common-Law Exceptions:
    i.   Trust

ii. Agency

iii. Restrictive Covenants

The above are just a few examples. So it is in real life. Unless you allow someone the right to access you, your personal space, and your state of being, then that person has no power, as a general rule, to *butt into* your life. That person has no power to change your moods or dictate your choices. Only those you choose should call you out, hold you responsible, advise you, and change the course of your destiny with their prayers, advice, actions, or inactions. So the primary question is, who have you given the *'right'* to influence your life? A second but equally important question is, who has access to your destiny?

"No Man Stands Alone"

For some of us, when we get to a particular stage of maturity, we are more willing to admit certain truths to ourselves. As we continue to grow, we become more willing to admit those truths to others. I believe it takes a different level of maturity to do either. Still, the latter may require just a bit more effort than the former. The truth is this; no one individual can survive on his or her own. God did not make us to withstand life's red tapes, hills, and valleys all on our own. Such a reality reminds me of a song/poem I learned in school entitled *"No Man is an Island."* The first stanza states:

> *"No man is an island*
> *No man stands alone*
> *each man's joy is joy to me*
> *each man's grief is my own..."*

The writer and I agree wholeheartedly on this. No one *'man'* can do this thing called life alone. However, whether we allow this knowledge to build us or break us is a separate matter. We must enforce a balance here if we are to grasp the concept of self-reliance and *"get help now before you crash and burn!"* On the one hand, we have to limit just how much we rely on others and how much others know we depend on them.

Sometimes, their knowledge of our reliance on them may give them a sense of power over another. A wise person can determine when to accept help and when to turn it down. There are many people with good hearts, but there are others who seek only to insert themselves into our lives so our lives will either be like the life they never had or a life they believe is perfect.

As for them, they are the epitome of perfection...we are just learning the meaning of the word. However, as Albert Einstein said, *"I am thankful for those who said no. Because of them, I did it myself."*

Sometimes, the answer *"no"* must come from us. It will come from others, certainly, but we have to know when to say *"no...I think I've got this."*

The difficulty most of us face is determining when to say *"no"* to the third party or external force and when to accept the help. Some offers often sound so helpful, so much like what you want to hear and need at that moment. However, time and again, we discover that the 'helping hand' will neither make you a better person nor make your situation any better. It may even impact your journey negatively. The importance of balance in our daily walk is once again evident, as is the reality that life will continue to be a puzzle none of us can ever solve. This fact makes it extremely interesting.

Now, *"No Man is an Island"* did not miraculously transform my tendency to be shy as a child or a loner. And even now, it has not wholly altered my introverted tendencies. It did, however, cause me to rethink my ways just a little bit, sometimes just a little too much. In doing so, I learned many life-changing lessons. The most important one has been the question of who I allow to impact my life. The question of influence is worth thinking about because whoever that is, there goes your control room, your power source, and the heart of the matter. Without a doubt, when we open our hearts to friends, family, church brothers, and sisters, or even colleagues, we open ourselves up to possibilities of pain. I have learned in my latter days to choose my pain wisely if I can do so.

Contaminated

Often, my husband has laughingly said my fear of germs results from something that was drilled in me during my childhood. While I have no such recollection, nor do I admit totally to any such fear, I partially blame my healthy dislike for germs on a television show I watched while growing up, known as "Monk." The research that followed into whether bacteria existed in the form highlighted by the series undoubtedly increased this dislike. So, when I threw away a Scotch-Brite stainless steel scrubber we used for scouring pots a few times at home, my husband questioned my actions. I told him it was contaminated.

Later that day, he said that he thought my actions were premature; he believed we could have gotten many more uses from the scrubber. My so-called obsession with bacteria and germs came up during that discussion. However, at the time, and even now, I believed I needed to discard the thing!

While I admit there are things in our lives that we need to throw out in a hurry, we have to be mindful that we do not discard items and persons who add value and meaning to our lives. As humans, we are inclined to measure others by a similar standard as we use to judge ourselves. This tendency can work for or against us. In order to protect your peace, the most reasonable removal includes persons who obtain unlimited benefits from our lives, with no liability for the selfish actions they may take in getting these benefits.

To protect and preserve friendships, I have experienced countless betrayals without doing or saying anything about it. Well, if one does not count posting statuses and pointed updates on Facebook and back in the days, Blackberry Messenger, then rarely did I say much. Very few people enjoy being the one who ruins what is seemingly perfect right? Not everyone wants to step on toes; some stepping may cause your physical and emotional demise, so once again, wisdom is the *woman* of the hour.

Eventually, my ability to confront selfish beneficiaries of my emotional generosity improved significantly. Still, starting conflict has never been something I enjoy. I continue to try my best to avoid conflict. However, even as I do, I now understand that some confrontation is often necessary. This lesson is vital when determining who or what to discard to protect your peace from third parties who should have no access to your mind. Like the devil who comes only to kill, steal, and destroy, brothers and sisters, on the road to who you are, I now know that many will come solely to contaminate your entire space.

While contaminants, like trouble, will come in various forms, one must either fight to thrive in the polluted environment, make it, or choose your departure time wisely. Some contamination is bearable; others are a glaring sign to exit stage right or stage left.

Notably, while you try to maintain serenity and peace with others, you have to be mindful of not stifling *you* to make others comfortable. I have been guilty of sacrificing my emotional healing to ensure that the semblance of perfect peace in a situation is maintained. It is a gut-wrenching feeling, wanting to explode, but for the sake of peace, you bite your tongue.

You cannot help your natural responses unless you acknowledge the flaws in them, admit you have flaws and then, adjust. Wounds left untended, even in the name of peace, can become the spark of dreadful wars.

Deny, Deny, Deny!

Denial itself is a contaminant that one often struggles with when perpetually trying to keep it all together. Sometimes, we have to allow ourselves to fall apart to figure things out, but again, ensure you fall into the right hands and at the right time. Lest we fall victim to the wrong person's opinion, to the wrong person's update, we must build resilience strong enough to resist the most dangerous bacteria in human to human interaction, which is unforgiveness.

People will hurt you; they will let you down, they will betray you, even those you love with your very being. Still, your failure to forgive them allows them rights to your very soul, something which happens without us even knowing at first. When the condition worsens and affects your physical health, it may come to your attention.

Unforgiveness robs you of the right to your joy, your smile, and hands it over to third parties. It controls the pace of your heartbeat when you are in the presence of your supposed enemies. It hurts your jaw when you have to force a smile, and it steals your serenity when a message pops up from these supposed enemies. It adds wrinkles, and it qualifies one for an extended stay in a red hot eternity.

When we give people rights to so much without the possibility of facing liability, the burden rests solely in our hands. Whether we hold ourselves liable for what we allow into our space and heart is an entire journey for which we must face the consequences. When we determine what is healthy for our peace of mind, we would be shocked to realize the things and people whom we handed over our peace to in the past. What is even more shocking is, most times, these people do not have a clue that your struggle involves their actions or inactions. What power we allow others and rob ourselves of, to our detriment. When one tries to reinvent him or herself, he or she must prepare for the fallout. But let no one, except the Lord himself, hinder the process of change. *Change must come.*

Questions of Rights:
i. What do we throw away that we could use for a higher purpose?
ii. What ideas do we abandon because of faulty reasoning?
iii. What do we get entangled with out of the desperate need to reach a goal?
iv. Is the person that the world sees daily the same person you meet in the mirror every day?
v. What are my hindrances, and how do I move past them?

Chapter 9

Ctrl+ Alt+ Delete (Control Issues)

"The greatest day in your life and mine is when we take responsibility for our attitudes. That's the day we finally grow up" – **John Maxwell.**

I believe that as humans, anything and everything can inspire us. This is why we must maintain the appropriate filters to our lives unless we prefer always to be engaged in battles for our peace of mind. I was compiling this book when I hit a combination of buttons labelled **"ctrl, alt, and delete"** to close a window that had become unresponsive. Several options popped up, which allowed me to determine the way forward for my device. Somewhere during that reasonably short process, my mind wandered into birthing an exciting title that could somehow fit into the diversity of ideas for this book. I later read the summary of another chapter of this book where I mentioned *"control issues."* Alas, this chapter came to the fore, slowly but convincingly.

A certain amount of pressure comes into play when one tries to ensure that nothing is out of place or that all things work together for good in *their* human strength instead of God's strength. This distinction is significant because, as most of us may accept by now, when we rely on God, even the harshest of circumstances become bearable. After all, we know that we are not on our own. The difficulty for me consistently arises when I try to do it all on my own, temporarily forgetting that I serve a great, big and wonderful God. This is compounded when one gets used to doing things on her own. You feel as if you are in control, as if you are indomitable in your own strength. Self-confidence is good. Overconfidence in self often leads to control issues, and so can your reluctance to ask for help. I am actively learning, though, that the more I let go of the ropes, rely on God to tell me when to sign off or switch users, and to cancel my subscription to unhealthy attitudes and people, the more I can trust the process and the one in charge of it. The process can be ugly, but the outcome, what a beauty it can be.

Switch Users

When you own a computer, you have the luxury of creating different access points. In doing so, the owner can sign in with one pin or password, and a guest or several guests can also sign in on the same device, using various codes. This flexibility means that your guests will not have access to your database of information, and you will not have access to their database. You have control over the number of guests allowed to access the device itself or to create a guest account on the said device. You have control over the entire machine. Whatever happens to that device, you have the final say.

I can look at this from several points of view. One, I have to know that except for God, I control my life, choices, and response to circumstances. Whether I want to admit it or not, my failures are mine; my weaknesses are my own. The refusal to accept this only screams immaturity and lack of personal development. So whatever I allow into my system, I have to handle. Whatever I refuse to accept, be it good or bad, I must also manage the consequences. Taking on what I had nothing to do with is a different matter. Based on personal experience, a decision to do so can be tiring and burdensome.

Similarly, I must choose whom I allow to access my system and how much access I allow when I do allow it. Taking back control of your space and life is essential but realizing when you deliberately or mistakenly gave away that control is also crucial. It is a critical balancing act that must be maintained when it comes to switching users. So like the matter of third-party rights, this area of your life requires a certain amount of intuitiveness.

I frequently remind myself of the need to allow God to take charge of the wheels of my life and not random people who come bearing an unlikely assortment of so-called *"gifts."* Know who steps to you for his/her own selfish reasons and know when you messed up and allowed the enemy to come into your court for all the wrong reasons. When you figure this out, do not be scared to hit that delete button. You can love without remaining tightly bonded to the things or persons who come only to cause you pain. One need not become a martyr for that which brings her no good and God no glory. Even as we take back control of our lives, we must also take control of our own choices and the effects of our choices.

Sign Off

Knowing when to call the game is very important. I found it challenging to let go of certain situations, friendships, relationships, and even jobs.

It is imperative that in the effort to get things right or to make things right, one does not overstay his or her time in a particular position. To everything, there is a time and season, says the word of God, a time to die, to live, to reap, to sow, and it continues. Suppose one is so invested in ensuring that a goal is met, despite the season for that goal passing. In that case, she will find herself drained while pouring into an ever-empty container full of holes. I reiterate, no one will get it right all the time, but this is crucial to peace of mind.

Have you ever given everything to a relationship that seems to go nowhere? Hanging around, waiting for change to come, for growth to take place, for him or her to decide to do better and stop torturing your battered soul, but the longer you wait, the more bruises you earn. Know when to hit that button and sign out or sign off. Protect your peace by closing the right doors in the right seasons. I have learned the hard way many times that only pain comes from overstaying your welcome in a person's life, at a place of business, in a friendship, or any situation.

Yes, lessons will come from the pain, and so will stories, such as this, but some lessons we could learn when we are more robust and in a better season. Not every lesson is to be understood while being battered and ripped apart emotionally or spiritually; some lessons we caused by our failure to discern seasons. Learn from other people's mistakes, other people's pain. You are not weak when you do this; wisdom dictates this. Signing off is not that bad. Christ used his short time on this earth to accomplish one task, which was to die for us. He came, he saw, he lived and died, and he conquered. Do what you must with whom you should and know when to sign off.

Laugh it Off (Cancel)

When I was in the second grade, a teacher said, in response to a classmate's belly bottom laugh at an inappropriate situation, *"He who laughs last laughs best."* I think that was the first time I heard that phrase in my then young life. Based on the context of her response, I made certain conclusions about what she meant. My seven-year-old self concluded that the teacher meant one must be mindful of who and what he/she laughs at, that laughter is unnecessary in certain situations. I also figured that she meant that one must be considerate in responding to others' circumstances because what goes around can come back around.

    I was literal as a child, mind you, and honestly, I can sometimes be very literal even now. Worry not, though! I have expanded my thinking, and I have a better understanding of the complexity of this simple proverb. Now, I realize that the adage not only addresses the literal meanings above. It is also a poignant reminder that the person who hangs around to the end, doesn't jump to conclusions, remains patient, and gives time for things to happen will get the better end of the stick. I have also realized that the person who is patient enough to wait until something happens before forming a conclusion can also maintain a peaceful state of mind. This person can better accept that *"anything that could go wrong will go wrong,"* but life continues. An individual who is at peace with life and has admitted that life will not always be a perfect unbroken line of blissful moments untested by failures will more likely shrug off these hurdles of life when they do appear.

For years, I restricted my smile and peace to moments of highs only, moments when I met my own unreasonably and almost impossibly high standards. These occasions were so rare; I found it difficult to determine in my head what the happiest days of my life were. Something was always not *"on point"* could have been better; something was still out of place.

I was tough on myself, and naturally, that made me harder on those in my immediate circle (a little harder ☺ in my head but way too hard, I have been told). I am still told today I am too hard on myself. Still, I have improved somewhat, allowing me to relax more readily, even if only a little more readily. Instead of going everywhere accompanied by frowns, anxieties, and doubts, I have been able to make a better habit of smiling even when I would prefer to wear the face of my moods.

When you frown more often than you smile, it is almost inevitable that people will form conclusions about your personality. For the extra intrusive ones, they may even form judgments about your emotional and mental state of being. I have been dragged down that road of conclusions on numerous occasions.

However, nothing changes your mind faster than personal experience or, better yet, a glimpse of what you look like when you frown more than you smile. I gained a new appreciation for mirrors when I entered the sixth form at my alma mater, so much so, the teacher who taught me Literature in English aptly renamed me *"mirror baby."* A second look in a mirror will tell you far more than the first glance ever can if you allow yourself to look beyond your reflection.

While laughter is not appropriate for all situations, I believe laughter is a cure in these circumstances. It cancels so many negative emotions that generally rise to the top when pain, hurt, anger, or fear is present. When we take ourselves too seriously, making an error, failing, performing at a subpar level will cause any smile to depart. But very few people can laugh and remain angry. We are not talking here about a woman scorned because that is a story for another day. Those women will laugh while smashing you to bits, but again, that is for another time.

Don't take yourself so seriously. Laugh at you, and when others join in, it won't hurt as much or at all. See the fun in more things. Have fun! Do something you've always wanted to do but were too scared or broke to do. Laugh more at the things and people who try to make things complicated. They will stop focusing on being a pain to you and focus more on why you are laughing at them or whether you are even laughing at them. Distract your detractors. The time they take to figure out your reaction and intention will leave them unfocused enough to forget about you and your problems and allow them a chance to figure themselves out.

Chapter 10

Growing in the Cracks

"Be your best you, just in case you have an audience."
Unknown Author

The truth is, our life is not only for us; we will always have an audience. Our audience will vary, but our purpose concerning the audience will never change. This simple purpose is to live our best life, and in the process, our stories may change many lives, hopefully, for the better. In my experience, I have never found greater peace than when I am making a difference in someone else's life other than my own. I do not advocate for ignoring your long-held dreams and goals. However, in attaining those goals, always remember that the world is full of people our lives were designed to impact.

Some may change one life. For others, it will be ten, and for a few, it will be millions of lives changed by their decision to live a selfless life. The number of lives changed is irrelevant; the existence of change is the key. After all the above, am I saying that life is better lived if you live to please others? NO. I am saying, after almost three decades on this earth, nothing brings me greater joy than seeing the world around me being a better place. Seeing others fed and at peace, being better than yesterday, growing, changing, and overall, living their best lives brings me even more joy. Sometimes, it physically hurts to observe the combative, aggressive, and unfriendly direction the world seems to go in. My eyes and ears, the doors to my inner being, have witnessed enough to painfully convert me into someone I would prefer not to be. But God!

Significantly fewer people will support someone they deem to be a direct competitor; many speak against another because they sense the greatness in that person. Greatness is not partial to one person. It is within all of us, but it cannot be uncovered if wandering eyes and distracted minds blind us. Nothing has ever been done or owned or created by merely wishing it were so. Change requires actions. Growth requires change. You never know whose next step or very survival depends on your endurance.

Ironically, the survival of those who make themselves into our enemies may just depend on you learning the lessons from your journey with that said enemy. This thought has scary implications, but the ability to grow in these and other cracks is essential for overcomers.

Growth in the Cracks

A few months ago, while my husband was busy

cutting the bushes that grew in the back of our yard, I, too, stayed busy watching him work. The yard was concrete, so the presence of the bushes was an unexpected reality for both of us. Initially, I had struggled with living in what I jokingly call the concrete jungle of Jamaica. I was born and raised in the so-called *'country'* with lots of shrubs, wooded areas, fruit trees, flowers, rivers, and an overall abundance of greenery. Bliss is what I call it.

But let me return to the soothing image of my husband, who was crouched down, making light of the weeds that grew between the cracks in the concrete surface. As I watched him, an idea surfaced in my mind; the possibility of planting edible items in the cracks! I have always wanted a backyard garden or farm, and this was a perfect opportunity to get back to something I enjoyed as a teenager while living in St. Thomas, Jamaica.

I shared the thought with my husband, brimming with excitement at the slight possibility. He chuckled and shook his head, murmuring in response, *"Only special trees can grow there, Monique."*
I laughed, undaunted by his doubts, and instead, quickly responded, *"nope, there is a crack there*

...anything can grow in that crack."

At that moment, my thoughts did an about-face. I smiled as the lightbulb grew brighter and more assertive in my mind, blooming from a seed to an entire tree in seconds. I looked at my husband and said to him excitedly, *"I have another idea for my book! Another chapter, at least. Growing in the cracks!"*
He looked up at me and laughed gently, *"Wow, you're something else, but I like it."*

And so came the birth of this portion of the book you are now reading. My husband often reminds me when discussing copyrighting one thing or another that *"ideas do not grow on trees."* Well, I would love to think those trees birthed something meaningful.

In difficult situations, which may be impossible for others, there can still be growth. Yes, it might take a different side of something to force the development, but growth is still possible. I observed that the trees grew everywhere there was a crack in our backyard. There were different trees, grass, and wild bushes, all of them shorter in length than usual. Bees were attracted to some flowers that grew through the cracks. So trees not only grew from those cracks, flowers grew. These flowers added a unique beauty to an otherwise green situation.

Lessons were springing forth from nature as I came to various conclusions. I observed that beauty could come through cracks, and the beauty of the growth attracted other life forms. It can be exhausting, scary, and discouraging to consider improving yourself in a challenging environment. It may feel easier to throw in the towel, but when nature sends me reminders of the possibility of progress even in tight situations, who am I not to run with the boost of courage it offers?

We will face obstacles in this life. Every journey comes with a story. Yes, we struggle differently, but we all struggle. Do not, however, become your struggle. Do not allow these melees to end everything you stand for. I find that my decision to continue to hang in there allows me to become a better version of myself and overcome myself. I can better cross hurdles I once found unsurmountable, and that means growth.

Dr. Myles Munroe said in one of his sermons and books, *"die empty!"* He concluded that the cemetery was a wealthy place full of books, cures for various diseases and viruses. He was preaching! I have since become absorbed with expending all that I have in me while I have the chance to do so.

Whether we believe in God or not, we cannot predict when or how we will die. However, we can affect how we die by wisely choosing how we live. In doing this, ensure that we live while we have the chance to do so. Do not die with your dreams, gifts, talents, and abilities tucked away in the corner of insecurity. I am preaching to myself even as I ring out this reminder to anyone who may be reading. No one but the enemy benefits from you failing to honor your time on earth.

Untangle the plans for your novel and dust off that old business plan you prepared five years ago. Remove that tracksuit from the bottom of your drawer and hit the gym! Get back around that computer and fill out the application form for your degree or certification! Send out those job applications, pack those bags and move away from that community. Book the ticket to go to Europe or Africa. Sign that agreement for sale and make that move into your first home. Finish your course well.

As you finish, take heart in the fact that God already knows how your story will end. In a television series, we witness the beginning of the character's story and the growing pains along the way. Many years later, we finally see the outcome in the series finale. There, we discover what happens to the character, whether he or she lives or dies.

Similarly, God has our story already written, edited, and played out in his mind. He knows every season of our lives and every villain that will come up, every star that will share the spotlight with us and then grow dim as they exit our lives. God knows every plot twist which may pop up because He wrote them all. He can tell when you need a mid-season break, and he knows exactly when to play the final season of your story. There will be many cracks along the way in this life, but with these reassurances in mind, *"becoming"* does not at all sound impossible, does it? No? So then, just do it!

Regret-LESS

Thinking over everything and wondering whether you made the right move results in one thing. Regrets. While it is essential to assess your actions, questioning every step, past, present, and future, will always leave you with regrets. Instead, we should be grateful for the experience and the lessons which we should try to learn from everything in this life. I wish I lived a life more grateful and less regretful. And even as I write, I am praying that I can do just that; live every moment with no regrets. Just live and be grateful

Women can well understand the cycle of pain. On a particular day, I was sitting around the dining table, typing away. I was having terrible back pain, and I could not give my best. I was constantly shifting and getting grumpier by the minute. Eventually, the pain became unbearable; I had to rise from the seat and change my location to a more comfortable couch. As I did so, my mind, ever so active, began to download how I could relate this to a book. Here I am, doing just that. I took so long to move because moving meant changing my position, leaving an area where I·felt somewhat comfortable.

Sometimes, we never know how much pain we feel until the pain passes. Sure, it hurts like crazy while it hurts, but when the pain passes, you realize all you could not do or missed out on because the pain distracted you from it.

Sometimes, you also realize the promotions and other possibilities you had to pass over because of the problem. Pain highlights everything negative around us. We see and feel the heat more; our anger burns hotter as our pain increases. Everything becomes more evident to you when pain is present. In the end, it is entirely possible to overcome the pain of regret and shift our focus to the possibility of hope.

Missed Opportunity or Not?

An opportunity for you at age twenty may not be the opportunity you want at age forty or may not be an opportunity at all. Things change, and so you may need to obtain a new skill set or mindset. You may have missed that opportunity, but it doesn't mean you have missed out on all opportunities. Trust me; if there is life, there are possibilities. Some people are holding on to your opportunities, and no, I don't mean they are *'badminding'* you as we say in Jamaica. I mean, you need to check that person and do business with that person. His or her ideas may make yours better. Do not stay stuck moping over missed prospects because the longer you stay stuck, the longer you stay not growing.

Do Life on Good Repeat

At the end of any day, one must adequately reflect on the past of that day. A day in any individual's life is full of enough lessons and stories to supply a publisher with books for decades. Even if you are of the mind that your life is as dull as a hundred-year-old eye of a legally blind man, take notes. Instead of merely going through a day, one would do well to assess the day carefully, the steps taken and those not taken, the turns made, and those desired. The friends made and the enemies made, the doors closed, and the doors opened must also be observed. It can be a never-ending process, but it is worth it.

When we start our lives, we often struggle with the questions, who am I? What am I? Or even, why am I? As we get older and hopefully wiser, if we give our close attention to our lives as we ought to, we discover who we are through the help of God and those he carefully placed in our lives. We also learn what we are, and we understand why we are. Who we are will never change. 'What' you are, this changes as you go through different life stages, and why you are will also change as you mature.

As I thought of the modern minds who may read this book, I do not doubt that many will challenge that our identity can change. Yes, a sex change can remove organs, hormones can change a body's shape, the tone of voice, and more, but the things that make us who we are, only God himself can change those, not men, nor women. Our true identity will always remain the same. This way, Christ can still identify us when he returns, even after we have replaced our faces, voices, or organs with those of another. I am Ann- Monique Ammoy Bailey Hutchinson, Norman, and Marlene Bailey's daughter, and those things can never change.

No one can undo what God has begun, and in creating us, He started a good work in us, and he who began a good work will bring it to the best end. We can determine what kind of ending we want by choosing our present moments.

So while our identity remains the same, our philosophies can change. As our philosophies change, so do our actions, and as our actions change, so do our lives. Our choices largely determine whether these changes are for the better or the worst. Are better or worst subjective? Some might argue that they are. Whether they are or not, our choices affect the final product our lives create. It is pertinent, therefore, that we choose well. We must figure out who we are and what we are and why we are and how we are. It is best if we do so earlier than later when life becomes so packed with everything and everyone, we have no space of mind to think about the essentials.

And even when life gets hard and trusts me, even for the financially wealthy, life gets hard; when it gets hard, you hang in there. You hang on for dear life because when you have life, you have so much hope! Hope changes things. So, we fight and hope and pray and do the best we can while we can.

Otherwise, God does have the final say. It makes no sense, therefore, to quit and give up and throw in the towel. It makes no sense we lay down and die, even though sometimes, it seems to be the easiest way out. Quitting is easy. Failing is easy. Doing nothing about anything is easy. Staying stuck is easy; being fearful is easy. Rising and surviving despite the odds, despite the struggles, despite illness, physically, emotionally, mentally, despite all the imperfections; that takes heart!

So yes, for those who have made it, even if you are now on your last try at this thing called life, take heart! One more shot is worth everything. Take heart! Rest today or tonight, wake up tomorrow and try life all over again. Even if you don't get it right tomorrow, sleep again and do it again until you've mastered the art of trying, living, fighting, and giving yourself a chance to survive without getting everything right, without being perfect in this world full of imperfections.

Reference

Maxwell, J. C. (n.d.). *brainyquote.com*. Retrieved March 30, 2020, from brainyquote.com: https://www.brainyquote.com/quotes/john_c_maxwell_125843

Baez, J. (n.d.). *lyrics.com*. Retrieved March 30, 2020, from lyrics.com: https://www.lyrics.com/track/406256/Joan+Baez/No+Man+Is+an+Island

Maxwell, J. C. (n.d.). *Good Reads*. Retrieved April 30, 2020, from goodreads.com:

https://www.goodreads.com/quotes/21752-life-is-10-what-happens-to-me-and-90-of

ABCNews. (n.d.). Retrieved 2020, from ABCNews.com: https://abcnews.go.com/International/bullied-teen-amanda-todd-leaves-chilling-youtube-video/story?id=1746326

Zafon, C. R. (n.d.). *Goodreads*. Retrieved 2020, from Goodreads.com:

https://www.goodreads.com/quotes/24450-the-words-with-which-a-child-s-heart-is-poisoned-whether

Goodreads. (n.d.). Retrieved 2020, from Goodreads.com: https://www.goodreads.com

Maxwell, J. C. (2012). *Developing the Leader Within You.* Nashville: Thomas Nelson Publishing.

Crosswalk. (n.d.). Retrieved 2020, from crosswalk.com: https://www.crosswalk.com/faith/spiritual-life/biblical-affirmations-to-heal-your-thoughts.html

People's World. (2015, July 31). Retrieved September 2020, from peoplesworld.org: https://www.peoplesworld.org/article/today-in-history-harry-potter-author-j-k-rowling-turns-50/

Made in the USA
Middletown, DE
16 May 2024